Gardener's ~~panion~~ to
EUCALYPTS

Gardener's Companion to
EUCALYPTS

Ivan Holliday and Geoffrey Watton

Published in 2002 by Reed New Holland
an imprint of New Holland Publishers (Australia) Pty Ltd
Sydney • Auckland • London • Cape Town
14 Aquatic Drive Frenchs Forest NSW 2086 Australia
218 Lake Road Northcote Auckland New Zealand
86 Edgware Road London W2 2EA United Kingdom
80 McKenzie Street Cape Town 8001 South Africa

First published by Rigby Publishers 1980
Reprinted 1983, 1985, 1987
Second revised edition published by Hamlyn Australia 1989
Reprinted 1995
Third revised edition published by Lansdowne Publishing Pty Ltd 1997
Fourth revised edition published by Reed New Holland 2002

National Library of Australia Cataloguing-in-Publication Data:

Holliday, Ivan, 1926- .
Gardener's companion to eucalypts.

4th ed.
Bibliography.
Includes index.
ISBN 1 87633 485 1.

1. Eucalyptus - Australia. I. Watton, Geoffrey. II. Title.

635.9773766

Publisher: Louise Egerton
Project Editor: Yani Silvana
Editor: Nicholas Szentkuti
Designer: Elaine Rushbrooke
Cover Design: Nanette Backhouse
Typesetter: Midland Typesetters Pty Ltd
Reproduction: Pica Digital, Singapore
Printer: Kyodo Printing, Singapore

CONTENTS

Acknowledgements

In compiling this new edition the authors were assisted in various ways by a number of friends and associates.

We wish to thank Dean Nicolle, Honours student at Adelaide University and noted eucalyptologist; Tekla Reichstein, Trevor Christianson and Martin O'Leary of the Adelaide Botanic Garden; Jennifer Gardner of the Waite Arboretum; Ian Brooker and David Jones of the National Herbarium, Canberra; Ross McKinnon, Curator, Mt. Coot-tha Botanic Garden, Brisbane; Colin Cornford of Brisbane; and Gloria Young, an Adelaide grower.

Special thanks goes to Beverley Watton for typing all of the additional species descriptions.

Photographic acknowledgments are:

E. alba (flowers)—John Brock

E. eremophila (tree only)—the late Brian Crafter

E. miniata, *E. ptychocarpa*—Merv Hodge

E. oleosa (flowers)—Dean Nicolle

E. phoenicea (tree)—Ian Brooker

E. phoenicea (flowers)—Dean Nicolle

E. pilularis (flowers)—David Jones

E. rossii (flowers)—David Jones

E. terminalis (flowers)—Colin Cornford

E. terminalis (tree)—Darrell Kraehenbuehl

Introduction

This book is not intended to be a guide to all the eucalypts of Australia, of which there are over 800 species as well as sub-species and some commonly grown hybrids. Several books have already been written which generally cover identification of the eucalypts as a whole, and these are essential references for both professional botanists and amateur enthusiasts.

Since this book was last revised (under the title of 'A Gardener's Guide to Eucalypts') L. Johnson and K. Hill of the Sydney Herbarium have published a paper in Telopea, Vol. 6 (2–3), which divides the eucalypts into two genera—*Eucalyptus* and *Corymbia*. *Corymbia* includes all of the Bloodwoods, such as the popular Lemon-scented Gum (*E. citriodora*), and some other species. In all, it covers 113 species, 33 of which are new.

For the present, however, *Eucalyptus* has been retained for all species described in this book. The authors consider that, as yet, there is not enough evidence to state that the change to *Corymbia* has been universally accepted. Any species which may become *Corymbia* in the future has been recognised by the inclusion of (*Corymbia*) with its title name.

The main purpose of this book is to provide an easy reference for the amateur to the eucalypts generally grown, or naturally common, in large cities and country towns, in streets, in private and public gardens, and along roadsides throughout Australia—i.e. those eucalyptus trees which the majority of Australians and visitors to Australia are most likely to see and inquire about, for ornamental or special purpose planting.

In the keys on pages 13 to 31 the species covered in this book have been arranged in broadly identifiable informal groups, such as roughbarks, those with blue foliage, and so on, in an attempt to assist the reader to more quickly identify species in the field. Within each group there is a non-technical key to guide the reader more quickly to the species. Species names, however, are arranged alphabetically to more readily assist those readers who may begin with the specific name and work from that direction.

In the descriptions in the text, an attempt has been made to give flowering time, but the reader should appreciate that eucalypts are not always predictable in this regard. Many of them produce flowers at odd times throughout the year, while others vary in the time they flower depending on the climate and seasonal changes, especially when cultivated in conditions different from their natural habitat. Thus a tree from Tasmania, for example, which may normally flower in summer in its home state, may flower at an entirely different time when grown in Adelaide.

It should be noted that eucalypts are notoriously variable within species. For example, although the bark of a species may usually be smooth and white, a form may be found with some rough bark; or a species normally with green foliage may occasionally appear in a blue-foliaged form.

Fruits, flowers and bud caps, too, may vary within a species depending on conditions and because some eucalypts hybridise naturally, often with an intergrading between species. The more species that are being cultivated, the more hybridisation is occurring between species growing in proximity to each other, resulting in subsequent hybrids of uncertain parentage.

It can be seen, therefore, that eucalypts are often not easy to identify.

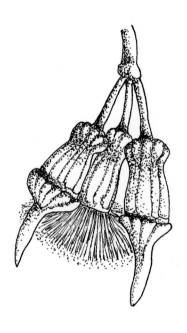

Features of the Eucalypt Plant

The diagrams on these pages are included to help people without botanical training understand the terminology used in the book. While technical terms have been avoided as much as possible throughout the text, there are some that have had to be used, and these are illustrated here. There is also a comprehensive glossary at the end of the book.

A Note on Eucalypt Leaves

Eucalypt leaves usually go through several changes before reaching their adult or mature form. These are shown in the accompanying diagrams of *Eucalyptus cladocalyx*.

At the seedling stage leaves are usually opposite for five to 10 pairs, sometimes bearing no resemblance to their ultimate shape. They then pass through a juvenile or secondary stage, and sometimes a further intermediate transition before attaining their final form. Species vary considerably with regard to the time that the juvenile foliage persists. Coppicing will often cause this foliage to return, and in some species — for example, *E. perriniana* — the attractive, rounded, perfoliate juvenile leaves can be retained indefinitely by judicious pruning.

CHANGES IN LEAF SHAPE *(E. cladocalyx)*

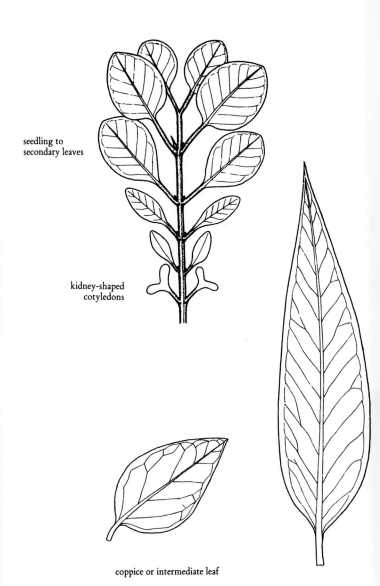

seedling to
secondary leaves

kidney-shaped
cotyledons

coppice or intermediate leaf

adult or mature
leaf (lanceolate)

0   1   2
cm

LEAF SHAPES

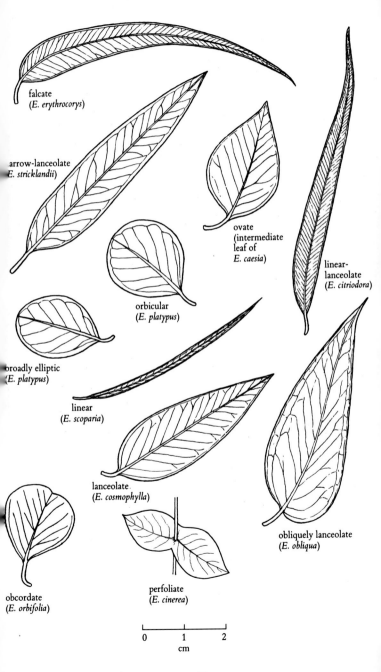

falcate
(*E. erythrocorys*)

arrow-lanceolate
(*E. stricklandii*)

ovate
(intermediate
leaf of
E. caesia)

orbicular
(*E. platypus*)

broadly elliptic
(*E. platypus*)

linear-
lanceolate
(*E. citriodora*)

linear
(*E. scoparia*)

lanceolate
(*E. cosmophylla*)

obliquely lanceolate
(*E. obliqua*)

obcordate
(*E. orbifolia*)

perfoliate
(*E. cinerea*)

0   1   2
cm

FLOWERS AND FRUITS

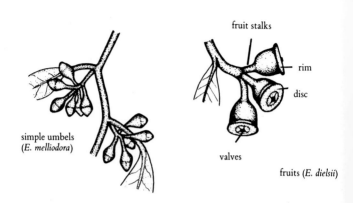

simple umbels
(*E. melliodora*)

fruit stalks

rim

disc

valves

fruits (*E. dielsii*)

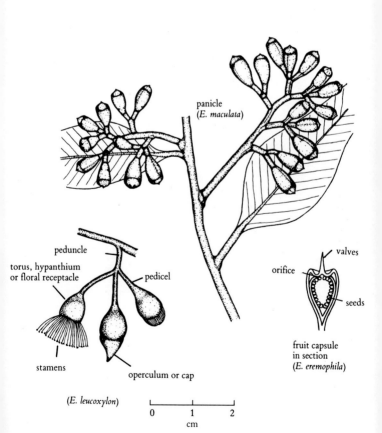

panicle
(*E. maculata*)

peduncle

torus, hypanthium
or floral receptacle

pedicel

stamens

operculum or cap

(*E. leucoxylon*)

valves

orifice

seeds

fruit capsule
in section
(*E. eremophila*)

0   1   2
cm

Keys

The following keys have been arranged to assist the non-technical reader to more rapidly identify a specimen, provided it is from a species included in the text.

For example, having found a tree with blue foliage the reader can quickly turn to Group 8 where the species can either be identified from the key, or narrowed down to a few species. These can then be examined against the alphabetical descriptions and photographs for positive identification.

In arranging the key, the authors have attempted to allot species to the group containing the more obvious identifiable feature. Obviously opinions will vary in some instances. For example, *E. macrocarpa* is included with those species featuring blue foliage (because this is a year-round feature), yet it may be its huge red flowers which attract the reader to discovering its identity and he or she may first look under Group 9— 'Eucalypts with prominent flowers or fruits'. In such cases, a cross-reference has been used from one group to the other.

GROUP 1—TALL SHAFT-LIKE FOREST TREES

The following species are mainly encountered in large gardens, parks and plantations, where their ultimate size is not a dis-advantage. Several are also quite commonly planted on small allotments, particularly the Tasmanian Blue Gum *(E. globulus)* and the Spotted Gum *(E. maculata)*. Eventually, however, these trees become too large for the small urban garden and they are generally not suitable for that purpose unless very carefully planned.

	species	page
Bark often striped, light tan to grey, with some rough patches; leaves large and leathery; juvenile leaves broad, blue for some time; bud caps beret-like, dimpled, glaucous; flowers and fruits single.	*globulus* subsp. *globulus*	120
Similar to the preceding but flowers and fruits stalkless, in threes, and smaller.	*globulus* subsp. *bicostata*	120

Similar to the above two but flowers in threes, peduncle thick.

globulus
subsp. *pseudoglobulus* 120

Bark rough at base, trunk smooth, white, bark rough brown when tree is young. Leaves large, glossy. Branchlets and buds often glaucous. Flowering time, autumn/winter.

grandis 126

Bark smooth throughout, grey, white or green in patches; flowers white, conspicuous; tree often more widely branching in cultivation.

maculata 160

Bark rough, fibrous at base; trunk smooth, white; old bark shed in ribbons; fruits small, pear-shaped, valves not protruding.

regnans 228

Tree almost identical to *E. grandis*, mainly differing in its fruiting valves, which are more erect and strongly outcurved; also its spring/summer flowering time.

saligna 126

Bark rough and grey at base; trunk and branches smooth and white; old shed bark hangs in ribbons; fruits hemispherical with domed, protruding valves.

viminalis
subsp. *viminalis* 286

GROUP 2—TREES WITH SMOOTH WHITE OR PALE GREY BARK

The smooth white-barked eucalypts, typified by the ghost gums, have captivated gardeners and photographers throughout Australia. Many of these trees exhibit pale grey or multi-coloured smooth bark towards the end of the yearly cycle, the bark deciduating to reveal gleaming white, or sometimes cream or salmon-coloured, fresh bark.

The large forest species usually have a stocking of rough bark at their base. These have been described in Group 1.

A. Medium to large trees
Bark powdery white, salmon pink to pale orange when new. Leaves ovate.

alba 32

Large graceful tree, foliage often sparse, leaves lemon-scented; bark pale grey to salmon when old.

citriodora 62

Large stately tree; fresh bark powdery white; juvenile foliage blue, persisting for some time.

dalrympleana
subsp. *dalrympleana* 238

Bark powdery white when fresh; sometimes with red patches when old; leaves narrow, foliage light; fruits small, rounded, valves protruding slightly.

mannifera
subsp. *mannifera* 162

Bark powdery white; foliage drooping; fruits papery, shed at maturity.

papuana
var. *aparrerinja* 196

Slender, medium-sized columnar tree; leaves very narrow (linear), dark green; branches often graceful, drooping.

scoparia 248

B. Small or slender trees

Usually straggly slender tree or mallee; bark powdery white, sometimes rough at base; flowers pale yellow, buds reddish, narrow, conical.

desmondensis 84

Small tree; bark powdery white when fresh (occasionally salmon); flowers conspicuous, bright red, or sometimes white, pale yellow, or pink, on long stalks; fruits long, bell-shaped, disc flat.

erythronema
var. *erythronema* 102

Flowers three per umbel; prominent collar around disc.

erythronema
var. *marginata* 102

Erect, slender, graceful tree of medium size; leaves very narrow, bright green; bark pale grey and white, sometimes with rough brown patches; flowers small, white, in thick umbels, buds club-shaped.

pulchella 218

Very slender tree, foliage sparse, drooping; trunk very thin, powdery white; fruits large, oval or urn-shaped.

sepulcralis 250

Similar to the above in mallee or multi-stemmed form.

pendens 250

Slender, medium-sized tree with umbrella-like crown; often straggly in cultivation; bark pale grey; flowers pale lemon, profuse; buds and fruits similar to *E. socialis* (see Group 10, caps hemispherical at base, narrowly conical thereafter.

transcontinentalis 284

Included elsewhere

E. grandis	}	See Group 1, page 14
E. saligna		
E. viminalis		
E. rossii		See Group 7, page 23
E. woodwardii		See Group 9, page 27

GROUP 3—TREES WITH SMOOTH BROWN (SOMETIMES SILVERY OR COLOURED) BARK (all Western Australian)

In Western Australia there are a number of small to medium-sized trees, some of them similar in appearance, which can be distinguished generally by their smooth, polished, brown or silvery brown bark. Among these are some mallees which can also be grown as taller single-stemmed trees. A few, such as the Silver-topped Gimlet (*E. campaspe*) and the Goldfields Blackbutt (*E. lesouefii*), display powdery white bark on the upper branches, a feature which enhances their overall appearance.

Within this group are included most of the yate or *Cornutae* group, two notable exceptions being the larger Yate Gum (*E. cornuta*) and the Tuart (*E. gomphocephala*) which are described in Group 4.

Some naturally growing small trees such as *E. newbeyi* may grow much larger under favourable conditions.

A. Trees of moderate (occasionally large) size

New bark tan or silvery, bark bitter to taste; branches erect.	*astringens*	40
Bark reddish brown to grey-white; buds in small clusters; fruits squat, globular, with narrow neck.	*brockwayi*	44
Foliage blue-grey; upper branches powdery white; buds spherical to conical, mealy white.	*campaspe*	58
Crown dense, spreading, low; flower head large, greenish yellow; bud caps smooth, finger-like.	*conferruminata*	68
Foliage often blue or purplish; flowers yellow; caps very narrow, horn-like.	*gardneri*	116
Small stocking of rough dark bark at base of old trees, not evident on young trees; upper branches powdery white; flowers white, bud caps and fruits prominently ribbed, glaucous or yellow.	*lesouefii*	146

Bark grey-brown; flower heads large, greenish yellow, bud caps long, warted; floral receptacle ribbed.

Fresh bark salmon-coloured, foliage very glossy, leaves small; fruits small, shed at maturity, bud caps mainly hemispherical.

Trunk often twisted or fluted, bark shiny brown; foliage very glossy; bud caps conical, obtuse.

Bark shiny brown, usually rough at base; leaves narrow; caps narrow, horn-like.

Old bark often green; leaves very narrow (linear); new buds usually red-brown.

Low bushy habit, flowers larger than in preceding.

B. Small trees, sometimes mallees
Bark greenish when fresh; flowers white, bud caps long, narrowing towards middle; valves long, narrow, prominently exserted.

Usually a neat bushy tree; flowers large, greenish-yellow; bud caps long. Similar tree to *E. newbeyi* but differs in its slightly warted, long bud caps and more rounded fruits.

Low dense tree; fruits flat-rimmed, cup-shaped; flowers yellow.

Bark shiny brown; buds and fruits two-winged, stalkless; flowers pale lemon or cream.

Variable tree, sometimes tall and sparse, sometimes a bushy mallee; bud caps long, horn-like, narrower than receptacle; flowers yellow, cream, sometimes brick-red, profuse.

Often a neat, bushy tree in cultivation; under natural conditions generally a shrubby slender mallee species. Bud caps are long, horn-like, smooth; flowers large, greenish-yellow. Fruits large, bell-shaped on flattened, curved peduncles.

Low dense tree; flowers dark red or cream; bud caps reddish, dome-shaped, narrower than receptacle; peduncles flattened.	*nutans*	182
Dense tree; leaves thick, orbicular to elliptical; flowers yellow (occasionally red); bud caps long, horn-like, peduncles flattened, deflexed.	*platypus* var. *platypus*	206
Similar to above with broad-lanceolate leaves; flowers white or yellow; fruits smaller than in preceding.	*platypus* var. *heterophylla*	206
Foliage very dense, numerous ascending branches; leaves stiff; fruits four-sided, winged; flowers white to pale yellow.	*steedmanii*	260
Similar tree to *E. newbeyi*. Usually a neat bushy tree; flowers large, greenish-yellow; bud-caps long and smooth, similar to *E. burdettiana* but differs in its generally smaller fruits and more to a cluster.	*talyuberlup*	178

Included elsewhere
E. stricklandii   See Group 9, page 28
E. macrandra   See Group 9, page 28

GROUP 4—ROUGH-BARKED EUCALYPTS

In general the rough-barked eucalypts have not gained as much popularity in cultivation as their counterparts with smooth or white bark. However, a number of species display a beauty of form and foliage which is very ornamental when coupled with the rough bark. In some species the distinctive bark characteristics very much enhance the tree's overall beauty. An added advantage to the gardener in using trees with persistent bark is the avoidance of the annual litter commonly produced by the deciduating smooth barks.

The rough-barked species included have been separated into two subgroups; those with persistent rough bark throughout, and those with rough-barked trunks but mainly deciduous smooth bark on the branches.

Some other roughbarks have been included elsewhere because of a more dominant identification characteristic, for example, the blue foliage of *E. cinerea*.

Group 4a—Medium to large trees with persistent rough bark throughout.

Bark finely fibrous, light grey but appearing white in sunlight; twigs and buds coated with whitish bloom.	*albens*	34
Bark dark brown to black, deeply furrowed; leaves grey-green, narrow; flowers in small panicles.	*crebra*	76
Tree similar to *E. crebra*. Bark softer, more flaky; bud caps are long and horn-shaped.	*fibrosa* subsp. *fibrosa*	76
Bark fibrous, dark grey to brown; buds green, large, club-like; flowers creamy white.	*gomphocephala*	122
Bark dark grey, deeply furrowed; foliage often blue-grey; fruits small, cup-shaped.	*largiflorens*	142
Bark grey, fibrous; caps often reddish, narrow and acutely conical; fruits almost spherical.	*marginata*	164
Bark mid-brown, soft, flaky; foliage bright green; fruits small, long, conical.	*microcorys*	174
Bark brown to grey, fibrous; leaves broad, glossy, oblique at base.	*obliqua*	184
Tree similar to *E. crebra*. Bud caps are dunce-like; fruits are larger with protruding valves.	*siderophloia*	76
Bark black or dark brown, deeply furrowed; foliage blue-grey; flowers pink or white, mainly in sevens, on long slender stalks.	*sideroxylon*	254
Similar to *sideroxylon* but with flowers in threes.	*tricarpa*	254

Group 4b—Roughbarks with deciduous smooth bark on most branches.

A. Medium to large trees

Rough bark dark grey, finely fibrous; leaves narrow, dark olive green; buds small, club-shaped; flowers white, profuse; fruits pyriform-truncate.	*amygdalina*	218

Branches ascending; rough bark brown, flaky-fibrous; leaves broad, glossy; flowers creamy white.	*botryoides*	42
Rough bark shaggy, dark grey; flowers yellow, prominent; bud caps long, narrow, horn-like; fruits in thick clusters, valves projecting, disc dome-like.	*cornuta*	72
Variable tree, usually large and gnarled when old; rough bark light grey, finely textured; flowers white, paniculate.	*microcarpa*	172
Erect, medium-sized to tall tree; rough, brown or grey bark, usually persisting over half to two-thirds of the trunk; upper trunk and branches smooth and cream to white; flowers white.	*pilularis*	202
Peppermint-type; bark rough, persistent, fine textured, grey; branches smooth, white or grey. Flowers white.	*piperita* subsp. *piperita*	224
Similar to preceding but a larger tree, differing in its distinctly urn-shaped fruits.	*piperita* subsp. *urceolaris*	224
Rough bark fine, fibrous; leaves long, narrow; buds club-like, profuse; flowers white; fruits ovoid, valves slightly below rim.	*radiata* subsp. *radiata*	224
Tree often small in cultivation; rough bark brown, thickly fibrous; leaves broad, leathery; caps pear-shaped, cream or pink; flowers prominent, cream; fruits cylindrical.	*robusta*	234

B. Small to medium trees

Rough bark grey, in fine strands; crown dense, often flat-topped; leaves very narrow, dark green, oily.	*cneorifolia*	66
Rough bark grey, fibrous; smooth bark red-brown; leaves narrow, glossy, deep green; buds long, conical.	*longicornis*	152
Erect tree; rough bark grey-brown, closely fibrous; leaves with prominent oblique lateral veins; caps hemispherical	*loxophleba* subsp. *loxophleba*	154
Mallee form of above; leaves thicker; buds and fruits larger.	*loxophleba* subsp. *gratiae*	154

Erect, often flat-crowned tree; rough bark dark grey, flaky; smooth bark white or cream; caps horn-like; fruits bell-shaped.	*occidentalis*	186
Medium to sometimes small or mallee-like tree; rough bark fibrous and chunky, dark grey to black; leaves narrow, dark green, oily; flowers in profuse umbels, white or cream, buds conical.	*odorata*	188
Rough bark, grey, short-fibred; leaves usually glossy, poplar-like	*populnea*	210
Mallee or medium-sized, often crooked tree; rough bark grey and scaly; leaves often light green; bud caps flatly conical.	*porosa*	212

GROUP 5—TREES WITH A PROMINENT STOCKING OF ROUGH BARK ON THE TRUNK

This is a group of eucalypts which have a stocking of rough or tessellated bark over the lower half or so of the main trunk. Thereafter the bark is smooth.
Eucalyptus melliodora is a widespread and variable tree which, although included here, may sometimes feature almost smooth bark throughout, or rough bark extending to the main branches.

Erect tree; bark on trunk dark grey, tessellated, smooth red-brown there-after; leaves narrow, lustrous; fruits small, cylindrical; flowers white.	*dundasii*	94
Medium-sized graceful tree, branch-es drooping; bark grey, cracked on lower trunk, smooth whitish there-after; leaves long and narrow; buds small, club-like.	*elata*	96
Erect tree; bark rough grey on most of trunk, smooth grey thereafter; leaves narrow; fruits small, hemi-spherical or pear-shaped.	*intertexta*	136
Large spreading tree; foliage often bluish; bark brown, fibrous at base, but variable; flowers small, white, sometimes pink.	*melliodora*	170

Tall, erect tree; bark cracked or tessellated, dark grey on lower trunk, smooth white or cream thereafter; branches drooping; fruits papery.	*tessellaris*	272

GROUP 6—TREES WITH MAINLY SMOOTH BUT VARIABLE BARK

A few species quite often seen in cultivation are difficult to categorise into any specific bark type. Among these, the Sugar Gum (*E. cladocalyx*) is one of the most commonly planted trees in Australia, particularly in farm and roadside woodlots of the moderately dry regions.

The River Red Gum (*E. camaldulensis*) is a very common tree in large parks and gardens in Adelaide and many country towns.

Large spreading trees; bark variable, usually grey and brown, patchy, sometimes white, particularly in dry locations.	*camaldulensis*	56
Large, erect branching tree; foliage very glossy; bark multicoloured, usually cream to yellow, orange and grey in patches.	*cladocalyx*	64
Similar to *E. cladocalyx* but lower, bushy-crowned habit.	*cladocalyx* 'Nana'	64
Low branching, dense tree; bark white, grey and pink; leaves thick; flowers and buds cream; fruits large, cup-shaped.	*cosmophylla*	74
Habit often irregular; small to medium tree; bark smooth, white, usually with many rough patches on trunk.	*fasciculosa*	106
Large, but variable tree; bark grey and white, streaky, sometimes rough on trunk; flowers mainly in threes, moderately large, white, yellow, pink or crimson, showy in good forms.	*leucoxylon* subsp. *leucoxylon*	148
Squat, dense tree; leaves, flowers and fruits larger than in subspecies *leucoxylon.*	*leucoxylon* subsp. *megalocarpa*	150
Recognised by its glaucous juvenile foliage.	*leucoxylon* subsp. *pruinosa*	150
Erect or straggly tree; bark sometimes rough on lower trunk, smooth tan and grey thereafter; fruits obviously conical.	*ovata*	194

Small to medium-sized tree; bark on trunk rough, brownish-grey at base smooth thereafter; foliage often willowy. Flowers profuse, red or pink, sometimes bright yellow or orange.	*petiolaris*	198
Large, upright tree; bark mottled grey or multicoloured; leaves glossy; bud caps long, conical, longer than torus.	*tereticornis*	268
Dense, low branching tree; bark mostly smooth, green; leaves broadly ovate, wavy, hairy.	*torelliana*	278
Erect tree; bark mottled, grey and white, sometimes yellowish brown; branches powdery; caps long, thin, conical.	*wandoo*	226

GROUP 7—SCRIBBLY GUMS—EUCALYPTS WITH SMOOTH WHITE OR GREYISH BARK MARKED WITH SCRIBBLES

A group of trees commonly described as 'Scribbly Gums' due to the outer bark of the smooth trunk normally having scribble-like marks, the result of the tunnelling action of insect larvae. Close examination shows that the scribble is in fact a double track.

Small tree, light irregular crown; smooth, white or pale grey bark marked by irregular scribbles. Flowers white; fruits cup-shaped, valves flat or convex, a distinctive red. Sydney region.	*haemastoma*	236
Small to medium-sized tree usually with a short bole and wide irregular crown. Bark deciduates to ground level in irregular patches or small flakes to show a smooth whitish surface, often scribbly. White flowers, fruit small, caps rounded or conical. Sydney region to near Brisbane	*racemosa*	236
Bark powdery white when fresh; old bark often scribbly; fruits rounded, rim flat, valves not protruding. Common in Canberra.	*rossii*	236
Small to medium-sized, often irregularly shaped tree; smooth white or greyish bark, often scribbly. Previously regarded as a form of E. *haemastoma* but adult leaves are		

narrower. White flowers and fruits are much smaller, more like *E. racemosa*. Sydney region.   *sclerophylla*   236

GROUP 8—EUCALYPTS WITH BLUE OR GREY FOLIAGE

Blue-foliaged eucalypts have always been popular in the garden because of the pleasing effect of their contrasting foliage. Unfortunately, there are several of the very large eucalypts, such as *E. globulus* (Tasmanian Blue Gum), which have attractive blue juvenile foliage and are sold in nurseries in this form. After a few years many unsuspecting gardeners find their 'Blue Gum' reverts to dark green, entirely different foliage, and ultimately grows too large.

The following list includes species which display blue foliage throughout their life span, although *E. perriniana* requires cutting back to retain this feature.

A. Medium-sized trees

Similar to *E. polyanthemos* (below) but buds conical or funnel-shaped.	*baueriana*	208
Bark dark, deeply furrowed; buds and fruits similar to *E. caleyi* but differs in its much greyer-green leaves.	*beyeri*	50
Bark dark, deeply furrowed; foliage silvery grey; fruits pear-shaped on long stalks; bud caps conical.	*caleyi* subsp. *caleyi*	50
Bark rough, pale grey or brown; leaves opposite, broad-lanceolate, intermediate leaves ovate, stalkless; fruits cup-shaped.	*cinerea* subsp. *cinerea*	60
Erect tree; bark smooth and brownish grey, rough at base; adult leaves small, alternate, stalked, ovate to lanceolate; juvenile leaves opposite, stalkless, rounded.	*gunnii*	132
Bark dark, furrowed; leaves silvery-blue, opposite, ovate, stalkless.	*melanophloia*	168
Bark rough, tree pyramidal when young; leaves narrow, new foliage plum-coloured.	*nicholii*	180
Bark rough, close-fibred; tree sometimes large and spreading; leaves broad, wavy, oval or round when young.	*polyanthemos*	208

Variable glaucous tree; bark smooth greyish grading to mealy white; juvenile leaves silvery blue, perfoliate, ovate-lanceolate to cordate; adult leaves elliptic to lanceolate, often purplish at tips; buds and flowers in many-flowered axillary umbels; fruits pear-shaped. *tenuiramis* 266

B. Small trees

Silvery blue, often pyramidal tree; bark scaly grading to mealy white; leaves rounded to ovate-cordate, opposite, sessile; flowers in threes; fruits globular or hemispherical-truncate. *cordata* 70

Leaves small, glaucous, edges crinkly (crenulate). *crenulata* 78

Old bark longitudinally curled, red-brown; buds and stems rounded, powdery white; leaves silvery grey, opposite, rounded, oval, or broad-lanceolate. *crucis* 80

Straggly small tree or mallee with prominent grey-blue to purplish blue foliage. Leaves broad-lanceolate. *cyanophylla* 82

Straggly tree; leaves broad, pointed, opposite, waxy blue-grey; buds long, conical; flowers yellow. *gillii* 118

Old bark longitudinally curled, red-brown; leaves round or obcordate; flowers yellow; bud caps pointed, faintly striate. *orbifolia* 192

Straggly glaucous tree; each pair of juvenile leaves joined to form a single orbicular or elliptic blade; mature leaves long, lanceolate; flowers in threes, buds conical; fruits small. *perriniana* 220

Slender glaucous tree, branches often horizontal; juvenile and adult leaves ovate to oval, stalkless, opposite; flowers in threes, caps hemispherical, beaked. *pulverulenta* 220

Slender tree, smooth brownish to green bark grading to mealy white; juvenile and adult leaves very glaucous, opposite, perfoliate, ovate-lanceolate to cordate; flowers creamy, in 7–20 flowered umbels; fruits pear-shaped, 6–8 mm across. *risdonii* 232

Similar to *E. orbifolia* but leaves small, obovate; fruits smaller.	*websteriana*	290

C. Very small trees or shrubs

Thin-stemmed tree or shrubs; leaves orbicular, stem-clasping; flowers yellow-green.	*kruseana*	138
Leaves large, silvery blue, ovate; stems and buds powdery white; flowers very large, bright red or pink or yellow, stalkless.	*macrocarpa*	158
Similar to above but leaves generally smaller, rounded or heart-shaped, flowers large, red, sometimes yellow, on prominent pendulous stalks.	*rhodantha*	230
Leaves large, oval, mealy blue to silver-grey; fruits and stems mealy white, four-sided; flowers white or cream.	*tetragona*	274

Included elsewhere

E. albida	See Group 10,	page 30
E. campaspe	See Group 3,	page 16
E. gardneri	See Group 3,	page 16
E. sideroxylon	See Group 4,	page 19
E. socialis	See Group 10,	page 31 (foliage not always blue)
E. tricarpa	See Group 4,	page 19
E. woodwardii	See Group 9,	page 27

GROUP 9—EUCALYPTS WITH PROMINENT FLOWERS OR FRUITS

Many of the eucalypts which have become established in cultivation have earned their popularity because of their spectacular or unusual flowers, or in some cases, their colourful fruits.

Some of these unfortunately do not generally grow into attractive trees, often forming straggly or sprawling specimens. However, if trained to grow into a many-stemmed mallee, or to a shrubby habit, they may often become an enhancing feature of the garden. This can sometimes be achieved by cutting a straggly specimen back below ground level. Numerous fresh stems are soon produced.

Not all of the species listed are like this: some are quite large upright trees.

A. Medium-sized to occasionally large trees

Medium to large tree, bark rough, fibrous; flowers pink or white in con-

spicuous heads, torus bell-shaped; fruits large, urn-shaped with constricted neck.	*calophylla*	52
Bark rough, yellow-brown, flaky; flowers snowy white or cream, caps beaked; fruits urn-shaped, narrow, sessile or slightly stalked.	*eximia*	104
Similar to *E. calophylla*, but generally a smaller tree; flowers vermilion, crimson or white; fruits without constricted neck.	*ficifolia*	108
Bark brown, short-fibred; leaves glossy; flowers white in large heads; fruits urn-shaped.	*gummifera*	130
Similar to preceding but fruits egg-shaped.	*intermedia*	130
Bark woolly or net-like on trunk, smooth and white thereafter; flowers orange, buds and fruits ribbed.	*miniata*	176
Leaves large; flowers in showy heads, red, pink or white; fruits cylindrical, ribbed.	*ptychocarpa*	216
Tree similar to *E. gummifera* although flowers are not as showy and fruits are smaller and more fragile. Bark is yellow-brown and flaky, tessellated.	*trachyphloia*	
Bark rough, yellow-brown, flaky. Bud caps shiny, light green, resembling a Scots beret. Flowers cream.	*watsoniana*	288
Tree often small and slender in cultivation; bark powdery white, branches pendulous; buds and stems powdery white; leaves glaucous; flowers bright yellow in thick clusters.	*woodwardii*	292

B. Small trees

Tree often slender; bark flaky, white, with rough patches; flowers large, yellow, caps bright red, biretta-like.	*erythrocorys*	100
Tree erect and slender, or shrubby; buds large, four-sided, red or orange, on long pendulous stalks, caps long, horn-like.	*dolichorhyncha*	114

Similar to preceding except caps bluntly conical or flattened hemispherical.	*forrestiana*	114
Tree straggly, leaves thick; flowers crimson; fruits stalkless, barrel-shaped, four-ribbed.	*lansdowneana*	140
Flowers smaller than above, white, mauve, purple or pink.	*albopurpurea*	140
Tree slender, often crooked; bark smooth brown; flowers yellow, up to 15 per umbel, caps red, long, horn-like; leaves with a dull sheen.	*macrandra*	156
Bark soft, scaly, persistent brownish on trunk and main branches, smooth and white thereafter. Spectacular, vivid orange-scarlet flowers arranged in a circular fashion around the peduncle.	*phoenicea*	200
Tree usually erect, slender; leaves thick; buds large, cylindrical, red, ribbed; flowers yellow.	*stoatei*	262
Bark smooth, brownish, powdery white on upper parts; leaves thick, glossy; flowers yellow, in thick clusters around branches, in summer.	*stricklandii*	264
Small to medium-sized tree, often several irregular trunks. Bark rough on lower trunk or throughout, tessellated. Flowers creamy white; bud caps white or cream; fruits large, elongated, urn-shaped.	*terminalis*	270
Crown dense, umbrella-shaped; bark dark grey, rough, scaly; flowers pink to red, occasionally cream; buds orange, ribbed.	*torquata*	280
Tree variable, sometimes of medium size, bark rough, scaly; flowers orange, yellow or cream in thick stalked umbels, variable.	*'Torwood'*	282

C. Very small trees or shrubs
Bark brown and longitudinally curled

on lower limbs, powdery white thereafter; flowers large, drooping, pink, anthers yellow; fruits powdery white, urn-shaped.

caesia
subsp. *caesia*   48

Similar to the above with larger, coarser leaves, larger deep pink, spectacular flowers and larger fruits.

caesia
subsp. *magna*   48

Similar to *E. tetraptera* (below), but fruits and flowers smaller.

erythrandra   276

Shrubby mallee; leaves thick, glossy; flowers large, yellow; buds bullet-like.

grossa   128

Shrubby mallee; flowers and fruits like *E. youngiana* (below) but smaller.

kingsmillii   294

Similar to the above but flowers red.

subsp. *alatissima*   294

Bud caps and fruits bright red, pointed, ribbed, on short stalks; leaves thick, erect; flowers cream.

pachyphylla   252

Low, shrubby mallee; flowers profuse, cream or yellow, torus long, conical.

pimpiniana   204

Shrubby mallee; leaves greyish, thick, leathery; flowers large, yellow, numerous; fruits bell-shaped.

preissiana   214

Fruit valves domed above rim.

var. *lobata*   214

Foliage bluish; bark smooth, grey; flowers large, red, pink, yellow or white, pendulous; fruits ridged.

pyriformis   222

Similar to *E. pachyphylla*, fruits stalkless.

sessilis   252

Untidy crooked tree; leaves very large, thick, leathery; fruits four-sided, red.

tetraptera   276

Untidy, bushy mallee, some rough bark on trunk; leaves thick, greyish; flowers very large, red, yellow or cream.

youngiana   294

Included elsewhere

Group 10—Some mallees not included elsewhere

Apart from those mallees already described in previous groups because of their flowers or other features, there are a number of other mallee eucalypts which are cultivated for specific utility purposes, as well as occasionally for ornament. These purposes include their general hardiness for windbreaks, and their ability to withstand difficult coastal conditions and poor limestone soils.

The list below is not exhaustive, but includes those species which, in the authors' experience, are more commonly grown.

Juvenile leaves broad, silvery grey-blue, returning after pruning; mature foliage narrow, glossy; flowers white, numerous along the branchlets.	*albida*	36
Leaves thick, mid-green, fruits barrel-shaped, thick, ridged. Close to E. *incrassata* but buds and fruits are larger.	*angulosa*	134
Buds large, rounded, ribbed, with narrow conical peak; flowers large, cream.	*burracoppinensis*	46
Leaves narrow, lanceolate; fruits four-sided, squarish; flowers white, sometimes pink; long flowering through winter.	*calycogona*	54
Dense straggly tree; leaves thick and stiff; fruits in tight, stalkless clusters, mainly hemispherical; caps conical, striated, squat.	*conglobata*	240
Slender stemmed mallee; smooth grey bark sheds in thin strips to reveal mottled grey and greenish-white smooth surface. White flowers occur in showy terminal panicles.	*curtisii*	92
Leaves dull, dark green; fruits hemispherical, slightly stalked; buds conical; flowers profuse, white; long flowering in winter.	*diversifolia* subsp. *diversifolia*	90
Bark rough and flaky at base, smooth grey or brown above, deciduating to whitish-cream. Profuse creamy-white flowers.	*dumosa*	92

Very similar to *E. socialis* but fruits and buds larger and powdery white. Younger leaves very glaucous.   *eucentrica*   256

Fruits prominent, urn-shaped; caps horn-shaped, slightly wider than torus; flowers showy, pale yellow or cream.   *flocktoniae*   110

Leaves greyish, wispy, terete or narrow-linear.   *formannii*   112

Fruits similar to *E. leptophylla* but smaller and valves at or below rim; buds club-shaped; flowers tiny, white.   *gracilis*   124

Leaves thick, mid-green; fruits barrel-shaped, thick, ridged.   *incrassata*   134

Leaves narrow; fruits small, cup-shaped, valves protruding in three sharp points; buds conical, often red; flowers white or cream, profuse.   *leptophylla*   144

Buds smooth, large, rounded with narrow conical point; flowers large, cream.   *oldfieldii*   46

Often a large mallee with rough bark at base; bud caps bluntly conical, narrower than torus; fruits rounded or pear-shaped with protruding needle-like valves.   *oleosa* subsp. *oleosa*   190

Usually small mallee; buds long, conical, pointed; flowers white or cream, very profuse.   *redunca*   226

Compact mallee; leaves thick, bud caps and torus ribbed, caps hemispherical with short beak.   *rugosa*   240

Foliage dull, usually greyish; bud caps hemispherical with long conical extension; flowers lemon yellow or cream, profuse; fruits pear- or cup-shaped, thin-rimmed, with sharply protruding valves.   *socialis*   256

E. alba Reinw. ex Blume

WHITE GUM, POPLAR GUM, SALMON GUM

DESCRIPTION: This common tree of the tropical north is very variable over its wide distribution and may grow as large as 18 m high but is often much smaller (to 10 m) with a spreading canopy. Bark is powdery white, but salmon pink when the old bark is first shed. The green leaves are ovate with prominent venation. These partly deciduate during the 'dry' season.

   The flowers are creamy white, occurring in the leaf axils in umbels of three to seven on a short peduncle, usually from May to September. The bud caps are blunt and rounded and the fruits cup-shaped or globular, with a thin rim.

OCCURRENCE: Widespread in the tropical north of Australia, from Western Australia across the 'Top End' to north Queensland, it is also one of the few eucalypts found naturally outside Australia—in Papua New Guinea, Java, Timor and other islands to the north. It can be found in thick stands inland and in places extends virtually to the sea.

CULTIVATION: A useful ornamental tree for the monsoonal areas, such as Darwin where it is cultivated as 'Salmon Gum'. Also a popular cultivated tree in other tropical countries such as Fiji.

E. albens Benth.

WHITE BOX

DESCRIPTION: White Box is a large, upright tree 25 m or more high, with a leafy canopy which gives dense shade. It is most easily distinguished by its finely fibrous, light grey bark which from a distance gives the impression of being smooth and white, especially when viewed with the sun shining on the trunk.

The broad-lanceolate leaves, twigs and buds are coated with whitish bloom which gives a silvery grey appearance to the tree. The buds are in tight clusters, either on very short pedicels or without them, on a small, erect peduncle. Caps are conical and flowers cream, appearing from summer to winter. Fruits are roughly pear-shaped or cylindrical with faint ribbing.

OCCURRENCE: A fairly common tree of the western slopes of the Great Dividing Range in New South Wales (including much of the wheatlands) and Victoria. It has also been recorded in the Wirrabara district of South Australia.

CULTIVATION: A good tree for shade and shelter on farms and for large parks. It is suited to most conditions in areas of moderate rainfall.

E. albida Maiden & Blakely

WHITE-LEAVED MALLEE

DESCRIPTION: A bushy slender-stemmed mallee species rarely exceeding 3 m in height. The feature of the tree is its blue-white juvenile foliage which is so often present on the lower branches at the same time as the slender, lustrous green, lanceolate mature leaves appear on the upper older branches. The oval juvenile leaves are opposite. Burning or pollarding of the branches will result in a return of juvenile foliage at any time in the tree's life.

The small white flowers which cluster thickly along the slender branches, usually in January, are also most attractive. Fruits are small and conical and the bark is smooth, a polished brown or grey-brown.

OCCURRENCE: A mallee of the open sandheaths of southern central Western Australia in the Tammin, Hyden and Newdegate areas.

CULTIVATION: A drought-resistant small tree which is easily grown in light or heavy soils in areas of low to moderate rainfall. A good tree for providing the florist trade with blue foliage.

E. annulata Benth.

OPEN-FRUITED MALLEE

DESCRIPTION: This neat bushy-crowned tree to 8 m high often forms mallee thickets in its natural habitat. The smooth-barked trunk is greyish, shedding to pale green or brownish yellow when the new bark is revealed. Mature leaves are dark shining green, narrow and alternate.

The white flowers are produced abundantly from spring to early autumn; they are stalkless and occur in umbels of up to seven. The long, cylindrical, often reddish bud caps narrow slightly in the middle. Fruits are cup-shaped, up to 1 cm across with exserted valves. A broad staminal rim at the top of the fruit gives the tree its specific name.

OCCURRENCE: South-west Western Australia from the eastern end of the Stirling Range to north of Esperance and north to near Norseman, where a slightly different form with short flower stalks is found.

CULTIVATION: A long-flowering, excellent honey tree, which grows rapidly and adapts to most soils in moderate to dry conditions.

E. astringens (Maiden) Maiden

BROWN MALLET

DESCRIPTION: A hardy medium-sized tree which can reach
20 m in height, but is usually 8–12 m, of upright stature
with an erect bole and fairly stiff umbrageous crown.
The bark is smooth and light brown or cream, and the
lanceolate, rather narrow leaves are grey-green, leathery
and alternate.

The flowers are mostly produced in the late spring and
early summer. These are creamy yellow, in umbels of up
to seven. The green operculum of the bud is long and
narrowly dome-shaped, with a blunt head. Fruits are
bell-shaped, about 12 mm long, with protruding triangular valves. Flowers and fruits bear, a close resemblance
to those of *E. occidentalis* (page 186), but the trees are
quite distinct.

A distinguishing feature of the tree is the bitter taste of
the bark, which gives rise to its specific name. The timber is very hard and durable.

OCCURRENCE: South-west Western Australia from north-
west of York in areas of moderate rainfall (380–560 mm)
southwards to Mount Barker and eastwards to
Ravensthorpe, on laterite or clay soils.

CULTIVATION: A hardy species for areas of low to moderate
rainfall, which is suited to most soils, including mildly
saline. Thrives in heavy, alkaline soils. Good honey tree.
Eventually kills plant life beneath its canopy.

E. botryoides Smith

BANGALAY, SOUTHERN MAHOGANY

DESCRIPTION: Usually a medium-sized tree with long, ascending but spreading branches, densely canopied towards the end of each branch with large, glossy, deep green leaves. The bark is dark brown, flaky, fibrous and furrowed on the trunk, extending to the lower branches, but smooth grey or light brown thereafter. The leaves are distinguished by numerous fine veins, almost at 90° to the midrib.

Flowers and fruits are almost sessile, carried in umbels of six to 10 on a flattened stalk (peduncle). The flowers, which normally appear in midsummer to autumn, are cream or white. Fruits are cup-shaped with the valves below the rim.

OCCURRENCE: In Victoria, from near Bairnsdale along coastal locations to the New South Wales border, extending along the south coast of that State. It is often found growing in beach dunes near the sea, as well as in better conditions further inland.

CULTIVATION: A hardy, easily grown tree which has been extensively cultivated, particularly near the sea and on swampy estuarine soils.

E. brockwayi C. A. Gardner

DUNDAS MAHOGANY

DESCRIPTION: Normally a shapely, broad-crowned, erect tree 10–15 m high, although occasionally specimens are found over 20 m high. The bark is smooth, reddish brown or salmon-coloured when fresh, greying with age before deciduating. Foliage is glossy dark green, the mature leaves alternate and lanceolate, with a thin curved apex.

  The flowers are small, usually cream, up to 13 per umbel, on short pedicels, the bud caps hemispherical. Flowering normally occurs in autumn. Fruits are globular with a short cylindrical neck, resembling a squat flower vase. The timber is red and durable.

OCCURRENCE: A tree restricted to the Norseman area of Western Australia, growing in sandy or gravelly loam. Rainfall is about 250 mm.

CULTIVATION: An adaptable attractive tree which is drought- and frost-resistant and suited to most soils including those containing salt. Requires temperate conditions and low to moderate rainfall.

E. burracoppinensis Maiden & Blakely

BURRACOPPIN MALLEE

DESCRIPTION: Normally a straggly, spreading tree or mallee, 3–6 m high, with rough, persistent bark on the main trunk(s) but smooth grey bark thereafter. The alternate leaves are relatively narrow, lanceolate, mid-green.

Appearing in late winter to December, the flowers are quite showy, up to 5 cm across and creamy yellow. The yellow-green bud caps are hemispherical with a narrow conical extension, and are faintly ribbed. The top-shaped woody fruits subtend a broad, cylindrical flat-topped disc with slightly protruding valves.

OCCURRENCE: A tree of the central wheatbelt of Western Australia, growing in heathland from just north of Merredin and Burracoppin south to the Kulin area. Also recorded from north-western South Australia.

CULTIVATION: Although not often cultivated, this tree has some appeal because of its flowers and its value as a honey tree. A good windbreak species for dry conditions.

E. oldfieldii F. Muell., Oldfield's Mallee, is a closely related mallee with broader, grey-green leaves and similar flowers which feature smooth, spherical flower buds topped by a blunt beak. It is a dry area species from the northern goldfields and wheatlands of Western Australia and is occasionally cultivated.

E.caesia Benth. subsp. *caesia*

GUNGURRA, GUNGURRU

DESCRIPTION: One of the small trees (normally 3–6 m high) associated with granite outcrops. Characterised by reddish bark curling off in longitudinal strands to expose smooth greenish brown bark beneath. Bark on the upper branches is mealy white, as are the fruits and buds.

A slender, open-crowned tree of weeping habit. The leaves are fairly narrow, lanceolate, with a mealy bloom on the stalks. Flowers appear in autumn and winter, a delicate pink or almost red, tipped with golden anthers, pendent in threes, on long mealy white stalks. Bud caps are bluntly conical and fruits are large, mealy white, and urn-shaped.

Several forms are cultivated including a very large-flowered tree of drooping habit, *E. caesia* subsp. *magna* Brooker & Hopper, sometimes sold as *E. caesia* 'Silver Princess'.

OCCURRENCE: A species found only among granite outcrops of Western Australia, at scattered locations from near Brookton east to the Fraser Range, with rainfall varying from 250 to 500 mm annually.

CULTIVATION: At its best a delightful small tree for the garden, with attractive year-round features including beautiful flowers over a long period. However, it does not always grow into a shapely tree and in such cases can be improved by pruning below ground level to produce a several-trunked mallee. Prefers non-limy soil and temperate conditions.

ssp. *magna*

E. caleyi Maiden **subsp.** *caleyi*

CALEY'S IRONBARK

DESCRIPTION: Usually a small to medium-sized tree, occasionally large, with silver-grey foliage and dark, almost black, deeply furrowed bark. The conspicuous, handsome foliage results from the alternate, broad-lanceolate to lanceolate, silvery leaves on long stalks.

The flower buds are also mealy blue-grey, the caps conical and pointed, narrower than the floral receptacle. Creamy white flowers appear in late autumn and winter in dainty axillary umbels or terminal panicles, arranged on a long slender peduncle. Fruits are smooth and pear-shaped, tapering to a slender stalk.

OCCURRENCE: Found on the north-western slopes of the Great Dividing Range north of the Goulburn River in New South Wales, extending into Queensland west of Warwick.

CULTIVATION: A lovely moderate-sized tree which is grown occasionally, but not to the extent it deserves. It is generally adaptable, but may not be suited to very limy soils. Frost tolerant and an excellent honey tree. A tree which merits more attention for garden cultivation.

E. beyeri, R. T. Baker, Beyer's Ironbark, has similar buds and fruits but can be distinguished by its much greyer-green leaves. A New South Wales species with, generally, a more southerly distribution.

E. calophylla R. Br.
(Corymbia)

MARRI, PORT GREGORY GUM

DESCRIPTION: A large, erect tree growing up to 50 m high under natural conditions, but seldom more than 20 m tall, with a dense canopy of heavy foliage, when cultivated. This species and the closely related but smaller-growing *E. ficifolia* (page 108) have long been in cultivation, and hybrids between the two occur.

Bark is rough, brown and flaky throughout, and the leaves are large and thick, with red-brown new growth. The large pink or white inflorescences are conspicuously displayed clear of the leaves, mainly in late summer, resulting in a magnificent flowering tree in the case of better specimens.

Fruits are large, woody and urn-shaped, with a constricted neck. This feature, and its larger size, bell-shaped torus, and generally larger leaves, help to distinguish it from *E. ficifolia*, which usually flowers earlier.

OCCURRENCE: A common tree of south-west Western Australia, but at its best in the higher-rainfall areas.

CULTIVATION: An extensively cultivated tree best suited to non-limy soils with assured moisture.

E. calycogona Turcz.

SQUARE-FRUITED MALLEE, GOOSEBERRY MALLEE

DESCRIPTION: Usually a mallee 3–8 m high, but occasionally a wide-branching single-stemmed tree to 9 m. The bark is smooth, pale grey, sometimes rough at the base of the trunk, deciduating in ribbons. Leaves are narrow-lanceolate, alternate and glossy. Bud caps are conical, sometimes with a narrowed point, and always shorter than the torus. The flowers, which usually appear in spring to early summer, are white or cream, occasionally pink. The distinctive feature of the tree is the squarish, four-sided fruits on short stalks.

OCCURRENCE: A widely distributed species of the mallee areas of Western Australia and South Australia, extending into Victoria.

CULTIVATION: A hardy, easily grown small tree suited as a windbreak, or occasionally used for ornament in garden plantations. The pink-flowering form is particularly attractive, when in flower.

This species has been separated into two subspecies and one variety by Nicolle (*Eucalypts of South Australia*, 1997).

E. camaldulensis Dehn

RIVER RED GUM

DESCRIPTION: This well-known Australian tree, made famous by Sir Hans Heysen's paintings, barely requires description. Under most conditions it is a thick-trunked, widely spreading, large tree with multicoloured bark, usually grey, off-white and brown, and mainly smooth. However, the tree varies considerably throughout its wide distribution, in the dry inland being found with pure white bark resembling the Ghost Gum (*E. papuana*—page 196). The name *E. camaldulensis* var. *obtusa Blakely* has been given to the northern form because of its rounded, more blunted bud caps.

Leaves are a dull grey-green, sometimes bluish, lanceolate to narrow-lanceolate and alternate. Flowering is irregular, the flowers being small and white. The bud caps are conically beaked in the southern form, but hemispherical or dome-shaped in the northern form. The small rounded or ovoid fruits have prominent protruding valves.

OCCURRENCE: Throughout Australia in all mainland States, common along watercourses.

CULTIVATION: Grown extensively in large gardens and parks of Australia, either as a planted or as a natural tree.

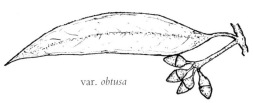

var. *obtusa*

E. campaspe S. Moore

SILVER-TOPPED GIMLET

DESCRIPTION: A small to medium-sized tree, normally 7–10 m high, often branching low on the trunk. The smooth bark is a shining coppery colour on the trunk, grading to powdery white on the younger branches. The trunk is sometimes fluted.

Leaves are lanceolate, grey-green to grey-blue, alternate. The greyish foliage combined with the bark is particularly ornamental. The fruits and broadly conical buds are mealy white and the flowers creamy white. Flowering usually occurs in summer. Fruits are hemispherical with slightly protruding, fragile valves. The timber is very hard and durable.

OCCURRENCE: The goldfields area surrounding Kalgoorlie in Western Australia, mainly on red loamy soils in association with Gimlet (*E. salubris*—page 244) and Salmon Gum (*E. salmonophloia*—page 242).

CULTIVATION: An adaptable, hardy, ornamental tree for dry to moderate conditions which is suited to most soils including those which are mildly salty.

E. cinerea F. Muell. ex Benth. subsp. *cinerea*

ARGYLE APPLE

DESCRIPTION: A compact and dense, low-branching tree which normally reaches 7–10 m high, distinguished by its permanent silvery blue foliage. The bark is rough, brown and fibrous.

Both intermediate and adult leaves and young branchlets are coated with a white waxy coating which gives to the tree its ash-blue appearance. Intermediate leaves are ovate, opposite and stalkless. Adult leaves are longer and lanceolate.

The buds, flowers and fruits occur in the axils of the upper leaves. Flowers are creamy white, usually appearing in summer and autumn. The bud caps are mealy white, conical, with a short beak. Fruits are also mealy white, small, and cup-shaped, the valves hidden below the rim of the cup.

OCCURRENCE: From near Bathurst in the New South Wales Tablelands north to Nerrigo and Gundaroo and in Victoria near Beechworth.

CULTIVATION: A frequently grown medium-sized tree which requires assured moisture and dislikes very limy or saline soils.

E. citriodora Hook.*(Corymbia)*

LEMON-SCENTED GUM

DESCRIPTION: This tall, erect, normally slender tree to 45 m high is well known for its smooth white, salmon, or pale grey deciduous bark, sparsely foliaged branches and lemon-scented leaves, the scent being particularly noticeable when the leaves are crushed. It is a true bloodwood, displaying leaves with a prominent midrib and parallel venation. The alternate leaves are long, narrow and lanceolate, and contain citronella oil.

Flowers are white and reasonably prominent, appearing from winter to summer in the southern States. The fruits, on short stalks, are urn-shaped and smooth, but sometimes have many rough protuberances on the surface.

OCCURRENCE: A tree of restricted occurrence in subtropical Queensland, between Mackay and Maryborough along the coast to 300 km inland. There is also a limited occurrence on the Atherton Tableland. It is closely related to Spotted Gum (*E. maculata*—page 160).

CULTIVATION: Despite its limited natural habitat, this is an adaptable, ornamental large tree which has been successfully cultivated under a wide range of soils and conditions in both Australia and overseas. It is inclined to drop branches without warning during strong wind storms.

E. cladocalyx F. Muell.

SUGAR GUM

DESCRIPTION: Another of Australia's best-known eucalypts, Sugar Gum is a large, upright tree with ascending branches, each with a dense terminal crown of glossy, deep green leaves. It can reach 35 m at its best, with a thick, smooth-barked trunk, the mottled bark white or cream, with patches of orange, yellow, brown or grey.

Leaves are lanceolate, narrow to broad, and very glossy. The flowers, which occur in axillary or terminal umbels, are creamy yellow, usually appearing in summer. Fruits are more or less urn-shaped and the bud caps flat and beret-like.

OCCURRENCE: A South Australian species found only in the southern Flinders Ranges, on Kangaroo Island, and near Port Lincoln on Eyre Peninsula.

CULTIVATION: A particularly adaptable tree which has been extensively planted on farms and along roadsides throughout temperate Australia.

The Bushy Sugar Gum (*E. cladocalyx* 'Nana') is a smaller, bushier form of the species which is also extensively cultivated.

E. cneorifolia DC.

KANGAROO ISLAND GUM

DESCRIPTION: A large mallee, or often a single-stemmed tree, to 10 m high, with a dense, often flat-topped crown of dark green, very narrow, oily leaves, but apple green when producing new foliage in early summer. The bark on the trunk is mainly rough, persistent, fine-stranded and dark grey, but becomes smooth and grey-brown thereafter. Leaves are linear or linear-lanceolate, erect on the branchlets, giving the tree a distinctive appearance.

Because of the oil content of the leaves, this species is used for eucalyptus oil production. The flowers are white, in tightly packed clusters, with longish, bluntly conical bud caps. Fruits are hemispherical and stalkless. Flowering occurs mainly in late summer and autumn.

OCCURRENCE: Restricted to the eastern half of Kangaroo Island in South Australia, where it is very prevalent, with a small outlier on Fleurieu Peninsula near Victor Harbor.

CULTIVATION: An attractive and distinctive tree which should be cultivated more than it is. Easily grown on most soils, including limestone, under temperate conditions.

E. conferruminata D. & S. Carr

BUSHY YATE

DESCRIPTION: This species was until 1981 confused with the mallee *E. lehmannii* Schauer, both being considered different forms of the same species.

It is usually a short-trunked, very densely crowned tree up to 8 m high, and lacks the lignotuber that is a feature of *E. lehmannii*. The bark is smooth, light grey to grey-brown, and deciduous, sometimes with a little rough bark at the base. Leaves are broad-lanceolate to elliptic and rather short.

Apart from its distinctive bushy-crowned habit the tree is distinguished by its large and unusual buds and fruits. The buds are in large globular, finger-like clusters, green or brownish yellow, on a thick flattened peduncle. The flowers form a rounded greenish yellow cluster about 10 cm in diameter of 15 to 25 individual flowers, appearing in winter and spring. Fruits are in globular heads with projecting pointed valves, rather resembling the head of a spiked club.

OCCURRENCE: The south coast of Western Australia, including the offshore islands.

CULTIVATION: Commonly cultivated from Perth to Sydney and overseas, either as an ornamental, as a street tree, or for farm purposes. It often resents solid limestone and some other calcareous soils but it is unpredictable in this regard. Reasonably salt-tolerant.

E. cordata Labill.

HEART-LEAVED SILVER GUM

DESCRIPTION: Although under favourable conditions this tree may reach 20 m high or more, in cultivation it is normally seen as a smaller, often pyramidal tree supporting dense silvery blue foliage to ground level. The deciduous bark is scaly on the main trunk, grading to mealy white on the smaller branches.

Leaves are very glaucous, opposite and stem-clasping, rounded to ovate-cordate in shape. Buds and fruits are mealy white and stalkless, occurring in three-flowered umbels on a short peduncle. The hemispherical caps are much shorter than the torus, with a short beak at the tip. Fruits are normally about 1 cm long and across with sunken valves. The creamy flowers usually appear in late summer and autumn.

OCCURRENCE: A tree from south-east Tasmania, where it favours damp situations at altitudes below 700 m.

CULTIVATION: One of the most ornamental of the so-called silver gums, or those with silvery blue foliage, this tree is often cultivated in Hobart and in the cooler parts of Victoria and South Australia, being best suited to cool, damp situations.

E. cornuta Labill.

YATE

DESCRIPTION: Yate is a medium to large, well-branched tree 10–20 m high with distinctive dark grey, shaggy bark on the trunk and lower parts of the tree, but smooth thereafter. The leaves are narrow-lanceolate, with a dull bluish sheen.

Distinctive are the profuse, globular clusters of bright yellow, showy flowers and grey fruits with prominent, dome-shaped, exserted discs with extended, pointed valves. Buds are long, thin, and horn-shaped, in thick clusters. Flowering occurs in summer. The strong timber was once prized for construction work.

OCCURRENCE: A tree of coastal south-west Western Australia from near Busselton to east of Albany, where rainfall is normally in excess of 850 mm annually, although a smaller-growing form appears in the drier Stirling Range inland of Albany.

CULTIVATION: An ornamental and useful flowering tree particularly suited to coastal planting in wet or saline soils. It adapts to most soils and conditions and thrives in tropical areas.

E. cosmophylla F. Muell.

CUP GUM

DESCRIPTION: Cup Gum is normally a low-growing but widely branching tree, seldom exceeding 5 m in height, with a dense canopy of thick grey-green leaves. Under very favourable conditions it sometimes grows much larger.

The bark is mainly smooth, in grey and white tonings, some small rough patches persisting on the trunk when the old bark is shed. The thick, alternate mature leaves are broad-lanceolate, and stalked. Flowers are produced mainly in autumn and winter; the buds are cream, stalkless, in groups not exceeding three on a short axillary peduncle, and the flowers are creamy white. The hemispherical two-ribbed fruits which follow are large, up to 2 cm across.

OCCURRENCE: Confined to South Australia, Cup Gum is found only on Kangaroo Island (the northern half) and in parts of the Mount Lofty Ranges, to the south coast, favouring boggy, acid soils of low fertility. The coastal form has broader leaves.

CULTIVATION: A tree which is occasionally cultivated for its flowers and low branching habit. Best suited to cool, moist situations, but is reasonably adaptable to harsher conditions and is successful on the Adelaide plains.

E. crebra F. Muell.

NARROW-LEAVED RED IRONBARK

DESCRIPTION: A medium-sized to large erect tree up to 30 m high usually, with a regular crown of dull green or grey-green leaves. The bark is typical of the ironbarks—dark grey to black, hard, deeply furrowed, persisting to the smaller branches. It exudes a reddish-coloured gum.

The leaves are narrow-lanceolate and alternate, on thin stalks. The flowers are small, white or cream, produced in panicles towards the ends of the branches. Flowering varies according to location but normally occurs from winter to summer. Bud caps are bluntly conical and fruits ovoid, with hidden or enclosed valves.

OCCURRENCE: A widely distributed species of Queensland and New South Wales, extending from near Cairns to south of Sydney and inland west of the Great Dividing Range on a variety of soil types.

CULTIVATION: An attractive tree mainly suited to parks and large gardens where its regular habit and permanent, distinctive bark can be used to advantage. Adapts to most soils and climates, provided rainfall exceeds about 450 mm.

E. fibrosa F. Muell. subsp. *fibrosa*, Broad-leaved Ironbark, which features long, horn-like bud caps, and *E. siderophloia* Benth., Ironbark, with dunce-like bud caps, can be found in the Sydney and Brisbane areas respectively.

E. crenulata Blakely & de Beuzeville

SILVER GUM

DESCRIPTION: This is only a small tree seldom exceeding about 8 m high, with a dense clothing of glaucous leaves reaching virtually to ground level. It is distinguished by its small, stem-clasping, heart-shaped blue-green leaves with crinkly (crenulate) margins. The bark is slightly rough, thin, and grey or grey-brown.

The small white flowers are produced in crowded umbels in the upper leaf axils, but are not showy. Bud caps are rounded with a distinct pointed beak and the fruits are glaucous and ovoid, with enclosed valves.

OCCURRENCE: A rare tree confined to the Acheron River valley to the north-east of Melbourne.

CULTIVATION: An attractive-foliaged small tree for cool temperate areas of assured rainfall. It is grown in many areas of Victoria as a specimen tree in small gardens.

E. crucis Maiden

SOUTHERN CROSS MALLEE, SILVER MALLEE

DESCRIPTION: Characteristically a straggly or crooked small tree to 7 m high, with dense silver-blue foliage and powdery white bark on the smaller branches, buds and stems, but longitudinally curled, reddish brown, deciduous bark on the trunk. The leaves are sessile, circular to ovate with a heart-shaped base, and opposite.

Flowers are creamy yellow, on longish pedicels, in umbels of up to 11, the umbel joined to the branchlet by a longer and thicker peduncle. Bud caps are hemispherical to flat-conical and fruits are shallowly hemispherical with a slightly raised disc. Flowers usually occur in summer.

OCCURRENCE: Another of the Western Australian species associated with granite outcrops. It is quite rare, being found at scattered outcrops north-east of Southern Cross west to Kellerberrin and northwards.

CULTIVATION: A particularly ornamental small tree, often requiring shaping. It is easily grown in dry to moderate, temperate areas, adapting to most soils. Leaf-eating caterpillars are its main enemy.

E. cyanophylla Brooker

MURRAYLANDS MALLEE, BLUE MALLEE

DESCRIPTION: A multistemmed tree to 6 m tall with bark mainly smooth, but fibrous towards the base, and with ornamental grey-blue to sometimes purplish blue foliage. The leaves are dull and broad-lanceolate.

The cream flowers occur in umbels of normally seven to 11 flowers from winter to late spring. Buds are ribbed, the cap being hemispherical to conical and shorter than the torus. The ribbed or wrinkled fruits are cylindrical or cup-shaped and mainly less than 1 cm long.

OCCURRENCE: Confined to the Murraylands district of South Australia, where it is common from Allawoona to Renmark, and similar country over the border in Victoria.

CULTIVATION: An attractive small tree because of its foliage, and suited to a range of soils where drainage is good and rainfall is not excessive.

E. pileata Blakely, Cap Gum, from Western Australia with a small outlier near Cummins on Eyre Peninsula, South Australia, has similar but reddish buds, cream flowers and dull grey or bluish green leaves. An attractive mallee, requiring similar conditions to *E. cyanophylla.*

E. desmondensis Maiden & Blakely

DESMOND MALLEE

DESCRIPTION: This is a slender, often crooked or straggly, small tree with drooping branches, to 5 m high, or a several-stemmed mallee of slender habit, 3–4 m high. The bark is smooth, white and powdery, extending to the small four-sided branchlets, some rough, flaky bark adorning the base of the trunk.

The leaves are alternate, rather broadly lanceolate or elliptic, thick and somewhat glaucous. The small, conical, pointed buds are bronze or reddish, in thick clusters. They open to reveal yellow or pale lemon flowers, normally in spring, but flowering is irregular. Fruits are roughly bell-shaped on short stalks.

OCCURRENCE: A Western Australian species restricted to the vicinity of Ravensthorpe, particularly near Mount Desmond, and nearby eastern areas.

CULTIVATION: An easily grown, drought-resistant shrub or small tree, suited to limestone and most other soils in temperate, moderately dry situations.

In the opinion of the authors, ornamental specimens are rare in cultivation.

E. dielsii C. A. Gardner

CAP-FRUITED MALLEE

DESCRIPTION: A neat, bushy, dense-crowned tree up to 5 m high, or a mallee, with smooth, shiny brown bark grading to grey as it ages. The leaves are glossy green, alternate, linear-lanceolate on slender stalks.

The buds and flowers are in pendulous umbels of up to seven; the pedicels and peduncle are long and slender. Bud caps are dome-shaped, slightly wider than the torus, and the flowers are yellow, normally appearing in summer. The cup-shaped fruits on long stalks have a flat, overlapping disc, with slightly protruding triangular valves.

OCCURRENCE: The Salmon Gums, Ravensthorpe, and Lake King areas of Western Australia on clay soils.

CULTIVATION: An attractive, profusely flowering small tree suited to most soils in dry to moderately dry, temperate areas. Could be effectively used as a street tree and should be cultivated more often than it is.

E. diptera Andrews

TWO-WINGED GIMLET

DESCRIPTION: A small, thin-trunked tree to 8 m high, or a mallee with many erect slender stems. The crown is dense, with narrow, lustrous green leaves and the bark is smooth and shiny, copper-brown or green-brown in colour. Sometimes it is fluted.

The buds are the distinctive feature of the tree. These are attached to the branches, singly or in threes, without pedicels or peduncles; they have two wings on the torus and reddish, sharply conical caps. Flowers are cream to yellow, normally appearing in autumn to early winter. Fruits are two-winged, hemispherical, the valves protruding slightly.

OCCURRENCE: Restricted to dry woodlands of the Norseman area of Western Australia, extending east and south for 100 km or more where rainfall is 250–300 mm annually.

CULTIVATION: A hardy, attractive, drought-resistant small tree suited to moderately dry areas, and to most soil conditions including slightly saline.

E. diversifolia Bonpl. subsp. *diversifolia*

SOAP MALLEE, SOUTH AUSTRALIAN COAST MALLEE

DESCRIPTION: This is usually a dense, bushy mallee to 4 m high, but in places away from the coast, and especially on Kangaroo Island, it can be seen growing as an erect tree 8 or 9 m high. The bark is a smooth grey, deciduating in strips. Mature leaves are alternate, lanceolate, rather a dull, dark olive green.

Unlike many mallees, the species is quite recognisable from a passing vehicle. The buds are in stalked clusters arranged on a long peduncle, the caps conical. Flowers are white, produced profusely in winter and spring. The fruits are globular with a raised rim, the valves about level with the rim.

OCCURRENCE: A common endemic mallee throughout coastal regions of South Australia including Kangaroo Island, from about Beachport to near Ceduna, as well as inland.

CULTIVATION: A useful tree for coastal and windbreak plantings, which is suited to dense limestone as well as other soils. It is a useful honey tree with ornamental flowers in good forms (see inset picture opposite).

E. dumosa A. Cunn. ex Oxley

WHITE MALLEE, CONGOO MALLEE

DESCRIPTION: A shrubby mallee or small tree, usually 3–10 m high. The bark is rough and flaky at the base of the trunk(s) and smooth grey or brownish thereafter, deciduating to a fresh whitish-cream. Lance-shaped mature leaves up to 100 mm long by 10–20 mm wide, are a dull green, the tip often hooked.

The flowers are profuse, in creamy-white axillary umbels of up to 7 per umbel, the peduncle angular and the caps conical, yellow to lime green coloured, usually finely ribbed. The fruiting capsules, to 9 mm long, are mainly cup to barrel shaped, the valves projecting slightly beyond the rim.

OCCURRENCE: Widely distributed throughout the moderately dry areas of New South Wales, Victoria and South Australia, where it is very common.

CULTIVATION: An easily grown tree in temperate to warm areas where rainfall is 300 mm to 650 mm per annum. Suited to limy, alkaline as well as most other soil types. Sometimes used as a street tree in Adelaide.

E. curtisii Blakely & C. White, Plunkett Mallee, is a popular street tree in some areas of Brisbane. It is a small, slender-trunked tree, or mallee, which features showy panicles of pure white flowers above the foliage in spring months. Endemic to the Brisbane region, it is unrelated to all other subgenera of eucalypts. Adaptable and grown as far south as Hobart.

E. dundasii Maiden

DUNDAS BLACKBUTT

DESCRIPTION: This is an erect tree, 9–20 m high, with a straight, rough-barked lower trunk, but mainly smooth red-brown bark thereafter and a canopy of glossy foliage. The rough bark is dark grey and tessellated. Leaves are alternate, lanceolate or falcate, narrow and a lustrous deep green.

The buds, flowers and fruits are without pedicels, in clusters of up to seven on an erect peduncle. The caps are hemispherical, topped by an abrupt peak, and the flowers are cream with the stamens reflexed and form small globular clusters. Fruits are cylindrical with deeply included valves. The timber is hard and durable.

OCCURRENCE: A tree of the Norseman – Salmon Gums – Fraser Range area of Western Australia, growing on alluvial, sandy loam.

CULTIVATION: A handsome, drought-resistant, moderate-sized tree suited to most conditions where rainfall is under 800 mm, but intolerant of saline soils. Makes an excellent street tree in arid areas.

E. elata Dehnh.

RIVER PEPPERMINT

DESCRIPTION: A most beautiful medium-sized tree featuring leafy, drooping branches, an erect rough-barked trunk and smooth white bark on the upper trunk and branches. The rough bark is grey and scaly or tessellated.

The leaves are long and narrow, linear-lanceolate, and a mid-green in colour. As in many peppermints, the flowers are produced abundantly in dense umbels which appear as small balls of white stamens. The buds are club-shaped and the fruits pear-shaped in dense clusters supported by a stout peduncle.

OCCURRENCE: An eastern States species from the central tablelands and the south coast of New South Wales and eastern Victoria, favouring the banks of streams and moist, but well-drained, soils.

CULTIVATION: One of a number of medium-sized eucalypts which are in scale for home garden planting, it is particularly ornamental, but has not been often used for the purpose. Best suited to soils with assured moisture.

E. eremophila (Diels) Maiden

TALL SAND MALLEE

DESCRIPTION: A single- or multi-stemmed tree of mallee habit, 3–8 m high, with a dense canopy of relatively stiff foliage and smooth polished brown or pale grey bark. The leaves are narrow, lanceolate, grey-green or sometimes blue-green, and alternate.

The long, narrow, often reddish, horn-shaped bud caps are a feature of the tree, these being followed by quite showy flowers—cream through to bright yellow, or occasionally brick red. Flowering occurs in winter and spring. Fruits are longish, shaped rather like a wine glass, with slightly exserted valves.

OCCURRENCE: Widespread in the wheatbelt and goldfields areas of Western Australia, the tree appears in various forms, with several described varieties.

CULTIVATION: One of the best small eucalypts for cultivation, being generally hardy under a wide range of conditions, attractive in flower (in good forms) and an excellent honey tree.

E. erythrocorys F. Muell.

ILLYARRIE, RED CAP GUM

DESCRIPTION: Usually a slender or straggly open-crowned tree, 3–10 m high, with curved glossy lanceolate leaves. Juvenile leaves are ovate, rough and furry. The bark is smooth, white or grey, with some rough patches, particularly near the base, and is shed in small flakes.

The feature of this tree is its flowers. These are large, single or in umbels of two or three, 5 cm or more across, prolific, particularly at the top of the tree, at first greenish yellow, later turning bright sulphur yellow. The operculum is a red biretta-like cap which brightly contrasts with the open flowers to produce a spectacular floral display during the autumn months. Fruits are large, woody and bell-shaped with prominent ribbing. The timber is quite soft and brittle for a eucalypt.

OCCURRENCE: Illyarrie is restricted to a narrow coastal strip of Western Australia from about the Murchison River south to Dandaragan, usually occurring as scattered trees on limestone soils, with rainfall about 450 mm annually.

CULTIVATION: Easily grown in low to moderate rainfall, on most soils, but favouring those of limestone origin. Seldom forms an attractive tree and is mainly grown for its spectacular flowers.

E. erythronema Turcz.

LINDSAY GUM, WHITE MALLEE,
RED-FLOWERED MALLEE

DESCRIPTION: At its best this is one of the loveliest of all the small flowering eucalypts. Normally a slender-stemmed mallee to 5 m under natural conditions, it grows into a small, slender or spreading tree to 7 m when cultivated. The bark is smooth, pure white or sometimes pale pink or salmon, being covered with a talc-like powder. The leaves are small, rather narrow but thick, a deep lustrous green, or occasionally blue-green.

The flowers, normally produced in summer and autumn, vary in colour from cream through yellow and pink to intense red, but red is most common, and accounts for the tree's specific name. Fruits and flowers are pendulous on long stalks, caps and fruits are conical, and the fruits are ribbed.

OCCURRENCE: An inhabitant of the wheat country of Western Australia, in the Wongan Hills – Corrigan – Southern Cross area.

A variety, *E. erythronema* var. *marginata* (Benth.) Maiden, occurs to the north of Wongan Hills as far as Wubin. It is distinguished by an expanded flat ring around the rim of the bud and fruit, and the flowers and fruits occur always in threes.

CULTIVATION: An ornamental small flowering tree suited to most conditions in dry or semi-dry locations. Several chance hybrids of this species have appeared in cultivation, including those known as *E.* 'Urrbrae Gem' and *E.* 'Augusta Wonder', but good forms of the species are just as attractive.

E. eximia Schauer

YELLOW BLOODWOOD

DESCRIPTION: This is a medium-sized, erect but often slender tree to 15 m under natural conditions, but it produces a dense, well-branched crown when grown as a single specimen. It features fine, flaky yellow-brown bark and long, curved, dull grey-green leaves.

Appearing for about two weeks during late spring, the flowers are particularly showy. They are snowy white (occasionally yellow) in thick corymbose clusters displayed above the foliage. The fruits are large and urn-shaped, and the bud caps are hemispherical with a short conical peak. Flowers and fruits are sessile or on short pedicels.

OCCURRENCE: A New South Wales tree restricted to the Hawkesbury Sandstone soils within an 80 km radius of Sydney.

CULTIVATION: Yellow Bloodwood has been successfully cultivated in Adelaide on heavy red-brown clay soils and on limestone soils, rainfall about 600 mm. Otherwise its adaptability is unknown to the authors. It is frost-tender when young.

E. fasciculosa F. Muell.

PINK GUM

Description: Characteristically, Pink Gum is a small, irregularly shaped tree, often with several trunks, because it inhabits poor, infertile soils. However, under more favourable conditions, where it is sometimes found, it reaches 10 m high with a substantial trunk. As an irregular specimen it has ornamental value because of its shape, its slightly drooping foliage, and its smooth, mainly white fresh bark.

The leaves are dull, grey-green, lanceolate to broad-lanceolate. The small white flowers appear in clusters, mainly towards the ends of the branches, normally in the late summer and autumn. Bud caps are small and bluntly conical, and the fruits are pear-shaped with hidden valves.

Occurrence: Principally a South Australian species from the Mount Lofty Ranges, Kangaroo Island and the south-east, extending just over the border into western Victoria. It favours poorly drained acid soils.

Cultivation: An ornamental small tree for an informal garden specimen, especially if allowed to develop with several trunks. Best suited to non-limy soils with assured moisture, but adaptable.

E. ficifolia F. Muell.
(Corymbia)

WESTERN AUSTRALIAN RED FLOWERING GUM

DESCRIPTION: This heavy-crowned, rough-barked tree 8–14 m high is probably the best known ornamental eucalypt, because of its spectacular flowers which are normally produced in summer months. Colour varies from vermilion through various shades of red to white (some may be natural hybrids with *E. calophylla*—page 52). In good specimens these flowers can almost hide the foliage when fully out, in a magnificent floral display.

The leaves are thick, dull, dark green, parallel-veined with a prominent midrib, and the bark is thickly fibrous, brown or grey. Fruits are large, woody and urn-shaped, generally smaller than those of the Marri (*E. calophylla*) and lacking the constricted neck of that species.

OCCURRENCE: A tree of very restricted occurrence, found only near Albany in Western Australia, on sandy soils.

CULTIVATION: This beautiful flowering tree is cultivated throughout the world and has adapted to a wide range of conditions, including situations near the sea, but is not generally suited to tropical or subtropical areas.

E. flocktoniae Maiden

MERRITT

DESCRIPTION: Merritt is a slender mallee to 8 m high with smooth, light grey or brown bark and sometimes a little persistent rough bark at the base. The fresh bark is often light brown. Adult leaves are lanceolate, alternate and dark green, but the seedling leaves are opposite in pairs, at first linear and then elliptical to almost round and sessile with the leaf edges continuing onto the stem, wing-like.

The flowers are pale lemon or cream and profuse; the caps are rounded with long horn-like extensions and the torus is urn-shaped or almost cylindrical. The torus enlarges to form a smooth, narrowly urn-shaped or cylindrical fruit on a stout pedicel. Flowering normally occurs in late winter and spring.

OCCURRENCE: A widespread tree in south-west Western Australia in the wheatbelt and goldfields areas, mainly growing in sandy loam. The South Australian form from Eyre Peninsula is now considered to be a separate species (*E. peninsularis*).

CULTIVATION: A hardy tree for most soils and situations where conditions are dry or moderately dry and climate is temperate.

E. formannii C. A. Gardner

DESCRIPTION: A tree or mallee, 4–11 m high, with distinctive and unusual foliage (for a eucalypt). The leaves are very narrow (sometimes terete) and pale grey-green, giving a rather wispy appearance to the tree, which is more like some species of other Australian genera than a eucalypt.

Rough grey bark persists on the lower parts of the tree but the bark is smooth, grey and deciduous thereafter. Buds are conical on short pedicels and the flowers are white or cream, occurring profusely in summer. The fruits are hemispherical with triangular valves projecting slightly from the capsule.

OCCURRENCE: This is a Western Australian tree of very restricted occurrence to the north of Southern Cross in the Die Hardy Range – Pigeon Rocks – Mount Jackson area.

CULTIVATION: Cultivation of this tree in Adelaide has indicated hardiness in the conditions generally encountered in that city. A tree worth growing for its foliage.

E. forrestiana Diels &
E. dolichorhyncha (Brooker) Brooker and Hopper

FUCHSIA GUMS

DESCRIPTION: Fuchsia Gums are mallees or bushy small trees 1–3 m high, or sometimes erect, slender trees to 5 m. The smooth grey bark sheds in long strips to expose light brown fresh bark. Leaves are thick, rather small, lanceolate to oblong, with an abrupt point.

The trees are distinguished by their large, four-sided winged buds and fruits, which are bright red grading through to other autumn colours. These appear together on pendulous stalks in profusion over long periods in summer and autumn and are very ornamental. The stamens are yellow and the bud caps are shortly conical or flattened hemispherical in *E. forrestiana* and long, narrow and horn-shaped in *E. dolichorhyncha*. Until recent revision separated the Fuchsia Gums into two species, they were both subspecies of *E. forrestiana*.

OCCURRENCE: *E. dolichorhyncha* is restricted to an area adjacent to the Norseman–Esperance road, mainly between Salmon Gums and Grass Patch. *E. forrestiana* is found over a wider range to the east and the west of this area.

CULTIVATION: Easily grown, ornamental small trees, particularly suited to dry or semi-dry conditions. However, flowers and fruits are usually more profuse and colourful in light or loamy soils and open conditions. Hybrids between the two often occur in cultivation.

E. dolichorhyncha

E. forrestiana

114

C. dolichorhyncha

E. gardneri Maiden

BLUE MALLET

DESCRIPTION: Blue Mallet normally grows erect to 6–9 m
high with many branches ascending from low on the
main trunk, and a bushy crown of blue-green to sometimes purplish blue foliage. The bark is smooth and pale
brown, ageing to grey. Leaves are alternate and lanceolate, on a short stalk.

The distinctive feature of the tree is the clusters of very
narrow, long, horn-like buds (up to 11) on an erect,
flattened peduncle. These open in early winter to reveal
pale yellow flowers in profusion. Fruits are long and
cylindrical or pear-shaped, with valves slightly below the
orifice.

OCCURRENCE: In the Narrogin – Katanning – Kondinin area
of south-west Western Australia, often in dense thickets
of very slender trees.

CULTIVATION: An adaptable, rapid-growing tree for most
soils, in temperate conditions outside the high-rainfall
areas.

E. gillii Maiden

CURLY MALLEE

DESCRIPTION: A small tree of crooked or twisted growth, either in mallee form or single-stemmed, rarely exceeding 5 m in height. It features dull, waxy, heart-shaped to ovate grey-blue leaves which are most attractive. Bark is pale grey to grey-brown and smooth, sometimes with a few rough patches near the base.

The flowers, which normally appear in clusters in late winter and spring, are creamy yellow. They arise from the leaf axils on stout peduncles, the long, pointed conical caps and dull buds being bluish and waxy. The ovoid to spherical fruits on short stalks have protruding needle-like valves.

OCCURRENCE: Restricted to the northern Flinders Ranges to Lake Frome in South Australia and a few isolated occurrences near Broken Hill in New South Wales.

CULTIVATION: An ornamental small tree worth growing for its foliage and flowers, but requires training to a manageable mallee habit for best effect. Easily grown in most soils in low to moderate rainfall areas.

E. globulus Labill. subsp. *globulus*

TASMANIAN BLUE GUM

DESCRIPTION: A large, shaft-like tree to 60 m high under favourable conditions, although it is smaller and of crooked growth in some coastal situations. The bark is smooth except near the base, and of varying colour, normally grey, white and tan, more or less striped; it is shed in long ribbons.

At first the leaves are mealy blue, broad, opposite, and stem-clasping, the stems square-sided and glaucous. However, when the tree reaches about 2 m the leaves change to a dark glossy green, becoming long, narrow, and curved. Flowers appear singly from winter to late spring, and are a deep cream. The large buds, caps and fruits are glaucous and prominently dimpled.

OCCURRENCE: Principally a forest tree of south-east Tasmania, but extending to the islands of Bass Strait and some areas of southern Victorian.

E. globulus subsp. ***bicostata*** (Maiden et al.) Kirkp., Eurabbie, is closely related but it has smaller, stalkless flowers in groups of three. It occurs in north-eastern Victoria and southern New South Wales.

E. globulus subsp. ***pseudoglobulus*** (Naudin ex Maiden) Kirkp., Victorian Eurabbie, from south-eastern Victoria, features flowers in threes on a thick peduncle.

CULTIVATION: Noted for their rapid growth, these trees are suited to most temperate conditions, including coastal. Vulnerable to borer attack in cultivation.

E. gomphocephala A. DC.

TUART

DESCRIPTION: Tuart is mainly a large tree of open forests, reaching 40 m high under natural conditions, but seldom growing larger than about 10–15 m high in cultivation. Because it is often grown in coastal situations it is a variable tree in size and habit, featuring rough, fibrous, grey-brown or grey bark, light green thick leaves with a dull sheen, and showy white or cream flowers, usually in autumn and winter.

It is easily identified by its distinctive clusters of green flower buds with club-like heads and large, long, bell-like, stalkless fruits.

The timber is heavy and strong and useful for construction work.

OCCURRENCE: An inhabitant of limestone soils along the west coast of Western Australia, extending from north of the Moore River south to the Busselton area. It mainly occurs in open forest where rainfall is 750–1000 mm annually.

CULTIVATION: A commonly cultivated adaptable tree for limestone soils and coastal situations. It is mildly salt-tolerant and despite its relative high-rainfall habitat is drought-resistant. Often attacked by borers.

122

E. gracilis F. Muell.

YORRELL

DESCRIPTION: Normally a mallee up to 4 m high, or a small tree to 9 m with a slender trunk and an umbrageous crown of shining narrow-lanceolate leaves. It grows much larger in Western Australia. The bark is often rough near the base but otherwise smooth and grey to grey-brown.

The buds are small and club-shaped, with a rounded or flat conical cap, and are attached to the leaf axils by a short stalk. Tiny white flowers appear in autumn and winter, followed by ovoid to pear-shaped fruits. These are similar to those of *E. leptophylla* (page 144) but differ in the normally hidden valves and much narrower rim.

OCCURRENCE: Widespread in South Australia and throughout the mallee areas of Victoria, New South Wales and Western Australia.

CULTIVATION: A useful, and ornamental, hardy tree for windbreak and other purposes on farms and elsewhere in low to moderate rainfall areas. Excellent for limestone soils.

E. grandis Hill ex Maiden

ROSE GUM, FLOODED GUM

DESCRIPTION: Rose Gum is one of the very tall, shaft-like forest trees of Australia, reaching a height of 60 m at its best and featuring a smooth, powdery white-barked bole up to 2 m in diameter. A short stocking of fibrous grey bark is usually persistent at the base. The leaves are a glossy green and lanceolate, but broader on young trees, when the bark is slightly rough and brown.

The small cream flowers normally appear in winter in axillary umbels of up to seven on a short peduncle; the caps are flatly conicle. Fruits are pear-shaped or cylindrical with slightly protruding valves.

The timber is milled and is a valued hardwood.

OCCURRENCE: From just north of Sydney to south-east Queensland in the high-rainfall coastal belt, often on the edge of subtropical rainforest. Isolated occurrences also appear as far north as the Atherton Tableland.

CULTIVATION: A rapid-growing tree which is frequently cultivated as far south as Adelaide, where it grows successfully if water is assured. Under these circumstances it forms an erect leafy tree to 20 m high.

E. saligna Smith, Sydney Blue Gum, is an almost identical forest tree, differing in its fruiting valves which are more erect and strongly outcurved, and its flowering time (summer).

E. grossa F. Muell. ex Benth.

COARSE-LEAVED MALLEE

DESCRIPTION: Normally a low sprawling mallee or a small, straggly and spreading tree 2–6 m high, with rough, fissured grey bark extending to the smooth reddish branchlets, and broad, large, shining, thick leaves. The plant is coarse and rather ugly, but if kept to a dense, medium-sized shrub where the foliage hides the trunk and branches, it can be quite ornamental.

The species is unmistakable, featuring heads of large yellow flowers, and bullet-shaped, red-brown stalkless buds on a thick, round-sectioned peduncle. Fruits are cylindrical, stalkless, green or greenish red.

Flowering occurs from late winter to December.

OCCURRENCE: This plant is found in southern Western Australia, mainly in the Lake Biddy – Newdegate and Salmon Gums – Grass Patch areas.

CULTIVATION: A species with ornamental flowers which should be regularly pruned to maintain a dense compact shrub, suitable for screening and windbreak purposes. Hardy and easily grown in most soils. Has succeeded in Sydney as well as the more temperate parts of Australia.

E. gummifera (Gaertn.) Hochr.(*Corymbia*)

RED BLOODWOOD

DESCRIPTION: A tall, dense-crowned tree to 30 m high, or more usually a smaller stunted tree to 15 m high with gnarled branches under natural conditions. The brown bark is persistent, rough, fibrous and flaky. Leaves are typical of the bloodwoods, featuring parallel veins, prominent midrib and thick texture. They are glossy dark green and lanceolate.

The white flowers normally appear in summer and autumn in showy terminal corymbs, the buds club-shaped and the caps hemispherical to conical and much shorter than the torus. Fruits are large, urn-shaped, pedicellate, with enclosed disc and valves.

OCCURRENCE: An eastern States tree of coastal regions from just over the Victorian eastern border to Maryborough in Queensland, favouring poor sandy soils. Found in the Sydney area and the Blue Mountains. Common between Bermagui and Merimbula on the south coast of New South Wales.

CULTIVATION: An attractive flowering tree which is best suited to moist conditions and non-limy soils.

E. intermedia R. T. Baker, Pink Bloodwood, is a similar tree from the east coast with which *E. gummifera* naturally hybridises.

E. trachyphloia F. Muell., Brown Bloodwood, is common in the Brisbane region.

E. gunnii Hook. f.

CIDER GUM

DESCRIPTION: This ornamental smallish tree is normally erect to 12 m high featuring dense, bluish, small-leaved foliage, the very small, rounded, opposite and sessile juvenile leaves persisting for some time. These ultimately mature to stalked, ovate to lanceolate, alternate leaves 5–8 cm long. Bark is deciduous, persistent and scaly at the base, brown-grey to green thereafter.

The flower buds are sessile or nearly so in three-flowered umbels, the torus cylindrical or narrowly conical and the cap pointed or beaked. White flowers appear in summer followed by cylindrical to ovoid truncate fruiting capsules about 1 cm long.

OCCURRENCE: This distinctive tree, easily recognised because of its foliage, is confined to the central plateau of Tasmania, usually in damp, boggy situations at altitudes of about 700–800 m.

CULTIVATION: Suited to the cooler temperate parts of Australia where rainfall is assured. It is cultivated in the British Isles and elsewhere overseas, where it can frequently be seen in private gardens.

E. incrassata Labill.

RIDGE-FRUITED MALLEE

DESCRIPTION: This rather stiff mallee grows 3–7 m high with dull, thick, broad-lanceolate leaves and smooth grey to grey-brown bark which is reddish when first revealed after the old bark is shed.

The showy flowers, which occur from winter to summer, are cream or white, in up to seven-flowered umbels, on thick peduncles, the pedicels very short or almost absent. Both torus and cap are evenly ribbed, the cap topped by a thick, blunt beak. Fruits are cup or barrel-shaped, with faint or distinct parallel ribbing.

OCCURRENCE: One of the common mallees found throughout South Australia and western Victoria, and extending into New South Wales, mainly in sandy soils. It also occurs in the southern mallee heaths of Western Australia.

The larger, thicker-fruited mallee, formerly known in South Australia as var. *angulosa*, has been given species recognition. Intergrading occurs between the two species.

CULTIVATION: Easily grown in areas of low to moderate rainfall. Useful for planting near the sea and as a windbreak for farms.

E. angulosa Schauer, Ridge-fruited Mallee, is very similar but features larger and much more coarsely ribbed fruits and buds. It occurs on the southern tip of Eyre Peninsula and at Newland Head, Fleurieu Peninsula, South Australia. The Western Australian form is expected to be described as a new species.

E. intertexta R. T. Baker

GUM-BARKED COOLIBAH

DESCRIPTION: A variable tree depending on conditions, but usually medium-sized, umbrageous, erect or crooked, 10–15 m high, occasionally much larger under good conditions. The bark on much of the main trunk (or trunks) is rough, grey, and tough-fibred, but it is mainly smooth and pale grey or white thereafter. Leaves are narrow, a dull green or bluish green and alternate.

The club-shaped buds occur in clusters, often at the ends of the branches; the cap is short and conical. Flowers are white, normally appearing in autumn and winter. The fruits are ovoid or pear-shaped with the valves usually hidden below the rim of the capsule.

Timber is hard and durable.

OCCURRENCE: An inland tree usually found following watercourses and land subject to inundation. It is found in western New South Wales, with a few disjunct patches in southern Queensland, northern South Australia including the Flinders Ranges, southern Northern Territory and the Cavanagh Range of Western Australia.

CULTIVATION: A tough, easily grown tree for dry or moderately dry conditions, appreciating additional water if this is available. Reasonably salt-tolerant.

E. kruseana F. Muell.

KRUSE'S MALLEE, BOOKLEAF MALLEE

DESCRIPTION: Normally a straggly mallee or shrub 2–3 m high, sometimes (in gardens) a small tree of bent or crooked stature. The bark is smooth and brown, deciduating in flakes to reveal smooth greenish brown fresh bark.

It is the opposite, round, stalkless, blue-grey mature leaves which are the feature of the tree, being arranged very closely together, on mealy white branchlets. Clustered among the leaves, the greenish yellow flowers appear in autumn and winter and combine with the grey-white conical unopened buds to beautify the tree. Fruits are cylindrical or cup-shaped and glaucous.

OCCURRENCE: A species found to the east and south-east of Kalgoorlie in Western Australia on granite soils associated with rock outcrops.

CULTIVATION: If kept to a bushy shrub this is a delightful foliage plant for the garden, but if left untrained it commonly forms a spindly, unattractive, although unusual, small tree. It is easy to grow in most soils in areas of low to moderate rainfall, but may suffer from leaf-eating caterpillars.

E.brachyphylla, described in previous editions, is now considered to be a naturally occurring hybrid related to *E. kruseana.* They grow together under natural conditions.

E. lansdowneana F. Muell. & J. E. Brown

CRIMSON MALLEE

DESCRIPTION: A small, straggly, slender tree or mallee, 2–5 m in height. It is distinguished by its particularly showy deep crimson or rich pink (occasionally white) flower clusters over a long period between autumn and spring. It features a slender trunk and drooping habit supporting thick, shiny green to yellow-green leaves which are often curved (falcate).

The flower buds are often red, more or less sessile, on a thick peduncle, the cap short and conical. Fruits are shortly barrel-shaped, ribbed or angled, with a narrow rim. Both buds and fruits occur in umbels of up to seven.

Makes a better ornamental specimen if the tree is cut to ground level every few years to form several stems from the base.

OCCURRENCE: Endemic to Gawler Ranges, Eyre Peninsula, South Australia.

E. albopurpurea (Boomsma) Nicolle, Port Lincoln Gum. Formerly a subspecies of the Crimson Mallee, this is a larger, often straggly, but wide-branching tree or mallee, 4–12 m in height. It features flowers which may be a unique purple, pink, mauve or white, usually between autumn and spring.

OCCURRENCE: Southern Eyre Peninsula, especially near Port Lincoln, and the southern side of Kangaroo Island.

CULTIVATION: Both the above are easily grown on most soils, including limestone, in temperate areas of low to moderate rainfall.

E. albopurpurea   *E. lansdowneana*

E. largiflorens F. Muell.

RIVER BOX, BLACK BOX

DESCRIPTION: Along watercourses where it is common, River Box grows to large tree proportions, with an erect trunk and a spreading canopy of branches reaching 20 m high at its best. Under less favourable conditions, it may grow to only small, often stunted stature.

The bark is rough, dark grey to black, deeply furrowed and persistent to the smaller branches. Leaves are dull, blue-green to greyish green, waxy and alternate. Buds occur in branched clusters, mainly at the ends of the branches, the short caps being rounded or conical. Flowers are small, white and profuse, normally appearing in spring and summer. Fruits are cylindrical to hemispherical with hidden valves.

OCCURRENCE: Widely distributed along major streams and river flats of south-eastern Australia, often in association with River Red Gum (*E. camaldulensis*—page 56). A common tree of the Murray River and its tributaries.

CULTIVATION: A useful tree for cultivation, mainly grown on difficult, boggy sites. It is reasonably salt-tolerant and useful for saline estuarine soils.

E. leptophylla F. Muell. ex Miq

NARROW-LEAVED RED MALLEE

DESCRIPTION: This is a slender-stemmed mallee 3–4 m high, or a slender tree up to 8 m with dark, shining green, narrow-lanceolate leaves and reddish branchlets. The bark is smooth and grey, and sheds in ribbons to reveal reddish brown fresh bark.

Good specimens are particularly floriferous, the numerous small, conical reddish buds opening into masses of creamy white flowers, usually in autumn and winter.

Fruits are small, cup-shaped with a thick rim.

It is a good honey tree and the leaves are rich in oil.

OCCURRENCE: A widely distributed tree from the moderately dry, temperate mallee areas of South Australia, Victoria and south-western New South Wales and extending into Western Australia as far as the eastern goldfields. It also occurs in the foothills of the Mt Lofty Ranges in very stony, dry soils, and on Kangaroo Island.

CULTIVATION: An adaptable, easily grown, drought-resistant tree suited to all soils in temperate areas of less than about 600 mm rainfall.

E. lesouefii Maiden

GOLDFIELDS BLACKBUTT

DESCRIPTION: Normally an erect tree 10–12 m high with some rough dark flaky bark at the base of the trunk but smooth and brownish thereafter, grading to mealy white or glaucous younger branchlets. Leaves are dull green or greyish, narrow, lanceolate or falcate.

The buds, in profuse umbels on mealy branchlets, are also glaucous to yellow, prominently ridged, with conical caps which are distinctly wider than the torus. Flowers are cream, appearing mainly in spring, summer and early autumn. The fruits are cup-shaped or slightly conical and evenly ridged, at first glaucous, but ageing to grey.

OCCURRENCE: The Western Australian goldfields area from Menzies to Norseman and approximately 160 km to the east. A closely related tree from the Norseman area known as *E. pterocarpa* features smooth, almost white bark throughout but similar buds and fruits.

CULTIVATION: An easily grown tree on most soils in low to moderate rainfall areas. Young trees are particularly ornamental, having mealy white branchlets, greyish leaves, smooth brown-barked trunk and handsome buds and flowers.

E. leucoxylon F. Muell. subsp. *leucoxylon*

SOUTH AUSTRALIAN BLUE GUM, YELLOW GUM

DESCRIPTION: This tree varies greatly in size depending on soils, rainfall, and location. It can be an erect large tree to 30 m high, or, more commonly, a medium-sized tree to 18 m, or sometimes small and stunted. Furthermore, there are several forms in cultivation which differ from the more typical tree.

The bark is also variable, mainly smooth, white and grey-streaked, but some rough bark is often found at the base and sometimes higher up the trunk.

Juvenile leaves are opposite and blue (hence the common name) but these are soon succeeded by leathery dark green, stalked, lanceolate mature leaves.

The buds, normally in threes on long slender pedicels on a peduncle of equal length, have beaked, conical caps, opening in autumn–winter to reveal creamy white, pink, or almost crimson flowers. Fruits are usually ovoid to subglobular.

OCCURRENCE: A common tree of the Mt Lofty Ranges and east to Murray Bridge, as well as Kangaroo Island, near Wirrabara and Penola in South Australia. Also found in Victoria south of the Grampians.

CULTIVATION: A very adaptable tree which succeeds on saline estuarine soils as well as most others (see page 150 for further comments on other subspecies).

E. leucoxylon F. Muell.
subsp. *megalocarpa* Boland

LARGE-FRUITED SOUTH AUSTRALIAN BLUE GUM

DESCRIPTION: This is a coastal form of E. *leucoxylon* (page 148) which is distinguished by its larger fruits and flowers, general habit of growth, and broader, thicker leaves. It normally grows only 6–8 m high with a dense spreading coarse-foliaged crown and short trunk.

Good forms of this tree are noted for large and profuse, deep pink to red flowers which are most conspicuous from April to July. Flowers may also be creamy white, or yellowish.

OCCURRENCE: In South Australia mainly near the coast, in the south-east, and south-west Victoria.

CULTIVATION: A hardy tree of particular use for coastal sites, as it succeeds in beach sand, but requires some wind protection for best results. Sometimes used as a street tree because of its low spreading shape. Several different forms are now in cultivation.

E. leucoxylon subsp. *pruinosa* (F. Muell. ex Miq.) Boland is a tree, 6–20 m high, distinguished by its very glaucous juvenile leaves. In South Australia it occurs from the Barossa north to the southern Flinders Ranges, and near Bordertown, extending into Victoria as far east as Melbourne.

E. longicornis (F. Muell.) F. Muell. ex Maiden

RED MORRELL

DESCRIPTION: An erect and branching tree up to 30 m high but usually less, with glossy, deep green, narrow-lanceolate leaves. The bark is rough, grey, and finely fibrous on the trunk and lower branches, but smooth grey-brown or reddish thereafter.

Buds, flowers and fruits are on slender pedicels in an umbel on a peduncle roughly 1 cm long.

The bud caps are narrowly dome-shaped or conical, and distinctly narrower than the torus. Flowers are white or creamy-coloured, normally appearing in late spring and summer.

Fruits are broadly pear-shaped or almost globular, with slender protruding valve points, which soon fracture and fall off.

OCCURRENCE: A widely distributed tree of the Western Australian wheatbelt and goldfields areas, where rainfall ranges from 200 to 500 mm.

CULTIVATION: Red Morrell is a tough, hardy tree which is drought- and frost-resistant, reasonably salt-tolerant, and ideal for shade and shelter planting on farms and along roadsides.

E. loxophleba Benth. subsp. *loxophleba*

YORK GUM

DESCRIPTION: An erect or crooked tree, normally 6–12 m high, with a well-branched crown and rough, furrowed, greyish bark on the trunk and lower branches, but smooth and brown thereafter. However, different forms of this tree are known: a smooth-barked form occurs at the eastern extremity of its range. The leaves are lanceolate, with prominent slanting veins.

The buds and fruits merge into the pedicels, the fruits with the pedicels being almost horn-shaped and the buds similar with a short, round, sometimes conical cap. They are in umbels of up to 11 on a short peduncle. The flowers are creamy white and sweet-smelling, appearing in spring or occasionally through to autumn.

OCCURRENCE: A widely distributed tree of south-west Western Australia from the Murchison River area to the eastern goldfields and southward to near Ravensthorpe, mainly in open woodland of under 500 mm rainfall.

CULTIVATION: A hardy drought- and frost-resistant tree suited to most soils including those which are mildly saline.

E. loxophleba Benth. subsp. *gratiae* Brooker is a smaller or mallee form of the species with larger, thicker leaves and larger buds and fruits. It is found on the sand plains of the Lake Grace – Lake King area.

E. macrandra F. Muell. ex Benth.

LONG-FLOWERED MARLOCK

DESCRIPTION: Usually a mallee under natural conditions, but in cultivation mainly a slender, often crooked tree to 7 m high. The bark is smooth and brown but ages to grey before deciduating. Leaves are lanceolate, thick, green to blue-green with a dull metallic sheen.

It is distinguished by its long, narrow, horn-like bud caps. The flower buds are in densely clustered umbels of up to 15. Flowers are yellow and profuse, appearing in late summer and early autumn. They are followed by clusters of cup-shaped fruits on a slightly flattened peduncle.

OCCURRENCE: A mallee often found in thickets in moist depressions and along streams, from the Stirling and Porongurup Ranges eastwards to the Phillips River in Western Australia.

CULTIVATION: Best grown as a mallee or several trees together. Hardy and successful in coastal situations and on salty estuarine soils, and particularly useful for this purpose. Cultivated in California as a small flowering tree, the bright yellow flowers being particularly ornamental.

E. macrocarpa Hook.

MOTTLECAH, ROSE OF THE WEST

DESCRIPTION: A spreading, straggly mallee or small crooked tree usually 2–4 m high, featuring large, broad, ovate to elliptic, silvery grey-blue stalkless leaves and powdery white, angular branchlets.

The single flowers and fruits are also distinctive. Buds are mealy grey on a thick peduncle, the cap more or less conical, and the flowers are bright red or pink, occasionally yellow, with yellow anthers and up to 10 cm across. The fruit is large, woody, flat, and top-shaped.

Flowering normally occurs in spring and summer, but isolated flowers can appear at any time throughout the year.

OCCURRENCE: A plant of the Western Australian sand heaths extending from near Geraldton in the north to Kulin in the south, in the 380–500 mm rainfall range.

CULTIVATION: Commonly cultivated because of its foliage and flowers. It is best suited to light well-drained soils, but adapts to heavier soils, requiring some training to develop a good shape, and protection from leaf-eating caterpillars. A prostrate form is also in cultivation. There is a subspecies *elachantha* Brooker & Hopper, which differs in its smaller stature, leaves and floral parts.

E. maculata Hook *(Corymbia)*

SPOTTED GUM

DESCRIPTION: This is a tall, erect tree with a long, shaft-like, smooth-barked trunk, reaching 45 m high at its best. A feature is the mottled or spotted, clean grey-green or cream bark with dimpled dark grey patches. Sometimes the bark is almost white throughout.

The leaves are dark green, glossy, lanceolate, with a prominent midrib and parallel veins. Flower buds are in profuse clusters, usually reddish brown, with a short hemispherical beaked cap. The flowers are white but prolific, and quite showy on good flowering forms, usually appearing in winter and spring. Fruits are urn-shaped, green ageing to grey, with deeply enclosed valves.

OCCURRENCE: A widespread tree of the east coast from Queensland to eastern Victoria. Here the Spotted Gum forests are a feature of the landscape.

CULTIVATION: A very adaptable tree which succeeds throughout much of Australia except in the very arid areas. It is often grown in small gardens but is eventually too large, unless very carefully planned.

E. mannifera Mudie
subsp. *mannifera*

BRITTLE GUM, RED SPOTTED GUM

DESCRIPTION: This is a graceful, light-foliaged, medium-sized tree, normally no more than 10 m high, but attaining larger proportions in very fertile soil. The bark is smooth and powdery white for much of the year, turning pinkish red and grey just before it is shed in long ribbons during summer.

The flowers are small and creamy white, appearing in spring and summer. Bud caps are hemispherical with a short pointed beak, and the small fruits are rounded or ovoid, the valves projecting hemispherically.

OCCURRENCE: A common tree of the southern tablelands of New South Wales favouring poor, shallow, and rocky soils where drainage is good. It is common around Canberra, and is extensively planted in that city.

CULTIVATION: An ornamental tree which grows rapidly until it reaches about 8 m and then moderates its growth rate, making it a very useful tree for street and garden plantations. Best suited to non-limy, well-drained soils.

There are several subspecies under *E. mannifera*, all somewhat similar trees in general appearance.

E. marginata Donn ex Smith

JARRAH

DESCRIPTION: Affected in many areas by the 'Jarrah dieback' disease, as well as by regular fires, many of the Jarrah forests today are unattractive. However, at its best, Jarrah is a large, straight-trunked tree to 40 m or more high with the top half of the tree well-canopied with dark green foliage. Bark is dull grey, strong and fibrous, and the leaves are narrow-lanceolate with a prominent midrib.

The creamy white flowers are borne in umbels of four to eight and occur in great profusion on some trees. Particularly on young trees and those of stunted form in poor soils, the flowers make a magnificent show, usually in October–November. Bud caps are reddish and acutely conical, and the fruits are almost spherical with enclosed valves.

Jarrah timber is dark red, hard and durable, and valued for many uses.

OCCURRENCE: A common tree of the Swan coastal plain and Darling Range to the south coast in south-west Western Australia, mainly in areas where rainfall exceeds 750 mm. It extends from near Jurien Bay to the Albany district on the south coast, where a stunted mallee form occurs.

CULTIVATION: Although rarely cultivated, Jarrah is a natural inhabitant of Perth and other settlements in Western Australia, where old Jarrah trees can still be found in parks and gardens.

E. megacornuta C. A. Gardner

WARTY YATE

DESCRIPTION: Normally a slender, erect, rather stiff tree 7–10 m high, with smooth grey or brownish bark. Leaves are thick, elliptic to lanceolate, and moderately short.

The tree features pendulous stalkless buds in groups of three to seven on a curved strap-like peduncle, with long, prominently warted, gherkin-like green caps. The large yellow-green flowers are borne in profusion, usually in winter and spring; although attractive, they are inclined to be hidden by the leaves. Fruits are woody and bell-shaped, with a raised, convex, striated green disc.

This species has a close affinity with the 3 species described on page 178.

OCCURRENCE: Restricted to the Ravensthorpe Range of Western Australia with a recorded outlier in the Fitzgerald River Reserve about 64 km south-west of Ravensthorpe.

CULTIVATION: An easily cultivated small tree which is suited to most soils in low or moderate rainfall areas, including coastal situations. Good honey tree.

E. melanophloia F. Muell

SILVER-LEAVED IRONBARK

DESCRIPTION: A small to medium-sized tree, normally no more than 8–12 m high but reaching to 20 m or more in fertile soils. It features a silvery-blue canopy due to its juvenile to intermediate leaves usually persisting for its entire life. Bark is mid to dark grey, persistent and deeply furrowed.

The leaves are opposite, with a very short stalk, the silvery-blue rounded to ovate leaves rarely maturing to a glaucous lanceolate. Attractive cream flowers appear, usually in summer, in 3–6 axillary umbels, or small terminal panicles, on slender dainty stalks. These contrast beautifully with the leaves. The caps are mainly conical and the fruits small and cup-shaped.

OCCURRENCE: A widely distributed tree, mainly inland of the Dividing Range, extending from northern New South Wales to northern Queensland. On the inland slopes where soils are poor and stony it may appear in places as the only species.

CULTIVATION: A very adaptable ornamental tree which is successful from the temperate areas of South Australia to the drier inland tropical or sub-tropical areas of Queensland. It is tolerant of moderate frosts and is drought resistant.

E. melliodora Cunn.

YELLOW BOX

DESCRIPTION: This is a large tree 20–35 m high, with a rounded, spreading crown and a thick trunk. The bark is rough, persistent and friable over much of the trunk, extending to the lower branches, but is smooth and light grey to white thereafter. Often the rough bark is a distinctive orange-brown which helps to readily identify the tree. The lanceolate leaves are variable in colour, but are often grey-blue, which contrasts well with the brown trunk.

The small flowers appear in umbels of three to seven forming panicles at the ends of the twigs. They are cream (rarely pink) and profuse, appearing in spring, summer and autumn. The bud caps are conical and the fruits pear-shaped or cup-shaped with hidden valves.

OCCURRENCE: A common tree of the open woodlands of the Great Dividing Range through Victoria, New South Wales and isolated areas of south-east Queensland. It also occurs in the Grampians in Victoria. A tree of variable form over its entire range.

CULTIVATION: Mainly suited to large parks and gardens where annual rainfall is at least 400 mm. One of the best eucalypts for beekeepers. A very ornamental form of this species with narrow, wispy, drooping foliage and masses of creamy flowers has appeared in cultivation.

E. microcarpa Maiden

GREY BOX

DESCRIPTION: This is a small to medium-large tree with finely textured, fibrous grey bark on the trunk to lower branches, but smooth grey-brown bark thereafter. Foliage is dull, dark green or grey-green, on spreading branches, the leaves being lanceolate.

The creamy white flowers occur in branched clusters (panicles) in late summer to winter, the caps conical and as long as the torus. Fruits vary in size from about 4 mm to 7 mm long and wide, and are usually cylindrical to pear-shaped.

In South Australia this tree has been confused with *E. odorata* (page 188), but it can be distinguished by its paniculate flowers and bark of finer texture. It also has a close affinity with other species known as Grey Box.

OCCURRENCE: It is widely distributed inland of the Great Dividing Range from southern Queensland through New South Wales to Victoria and South Australia. A common tree of the western slopes of the Mount Lofty Ranges near Adelaide.

CULTIVATION: An easily grown tree which is not often cultivated, but included because of its natural occurrence in many suburban Adelaide foothills gardens.

E. microcorys F. Muell.

TALLOW WOOD

DESCRIPTION: This is a large erect tree 30–50 m high at its best, with a compact crown of rather distinctive, glossy pale green foliage. The brown bark is rough and persistent throughout, soft and spongy, fibrous, with corky patches. Leaves are alternate, broad-lanceolate, and sharply pointed.

Small but showy white flowers appear from winter to late spring in axillary and terminal panicles. The bud caps are conical and the fruits are long-cylindrical, with slightly protruding valve points.

Tallow Wood timber is prized for flooring and joinery and is milled for this purpose.

OCCURRENCE: Common in hilly or mountainous country near the coast in southern Queensland and northern New South Wales, where rainfall reaches 1500 mm annually.

CULTIVATION: A tree of handsome appearance which is best suited to deep moist soils but is successful in areas such as the Mounty Lofty Ranges near Adelaide.

E. miniata Cunn. ex Schauer

WOOLLYBUTT, MELALEUCA GUM

DESCRIPTION: This is a tree of variable size, 8–30 m high, often with wide-spreading branches. The bark on the lower trunk consists of numerous papery flakes which decay to persistent brown netting-like bark. Elsewhere the bark is a smooth white to powdery white on the smaller branches.

Leaves are broad-lanceolate and the flowers a bright orange or vermilion, occurring in three- to seven-flowered umbels in winter. The buds and fresh fruits are a powdery white or greenish colour and prominently ribbed. Caps are hemispherical and beaked, and the fruits long and cylindrical.

OCCURRENCE: A monsoonal tree from the north, extending from the northern Kimberleys in Western Australia across the Northern Territory into Queensland.

CULTIVATION: A beautiful flowering tree for the tropics, which is occasionally cultivated in Darwin, Brisbane, and other Queensland towns. It flowers well at an early age.

E. newbeyi Carr & Carr

BEAUFORT INLET MALLET

DESCRIPTION: Under natural conditions, this is a shrubby
or slender mallet species, but in cultivation often forms
a neat and compact, erect small 4–8 m tree, with a short
trunk and dense crown. The bark is smooth, light to
mid-brown, often with green patches. Leaves are small,
fairly narrow, alternate and lanceolate, 4–7 cm long.

The tree is a member of the Yate or Cornutae group
of eucalypts, displaying distinctive flower buds with
long, smooth, horn-like bud caps and large bell-shaped,
more or less, sessile, fruits up to 3.5 cm across, on flattened curved peduncles. The flowers are large, greenish-yellow, in groups of 3–9 on each peduncle. They
normally appear between September and February.

OCCURRENCE: Restricted to near Beaufort Inlet and the
Fitzgerald River National Park in Western Australia.

CULTIVATION: A useful, ornamental and adaptable, small to
medium-sized tree, suited to specimen or windbreak
planting in most soils, in temperate areas of low to
moderate rainfall. Used as a street tree.

This tree is closely related to the Warty Yate (page 166)
and to two other rare species, all four endemic to
Western Australia.

E. burdettiana Blakely & Steedman, Burdett's Gum, known
only from East Mount Barren, can be distinguished by
its slightly warted bud caps and more rounded fruits.

E. talyuberlup Carr & Carr, occurs only in a small area of
the Stirling Range and nearby. It also features smooth bud
caps but generally smaller fruits and more to a cluster.

E. nicholii Maiden & Blakely

NARROW-LEAVED BLACK PEPPERMINT

DESCRIPTION: This is an ornamental, erect, and usually narrow pyramidal tree 8–12 m high, which features grey-green to blue willowy foliage with pink to purplish new growth. The persistent bark is rough, fibrous, and grey-brown. Leaves are narrow-lanceolate and alternate, on short stalks.

The white flowers are produced in small stalked umbels; the bud caps are hemispherical with a short beak, or conical. Flowering normally occurs in autumn. Fruits are small and rounded with a convex, projecting disc, the valves exserted or level with the disc.

OCCURRENCE: Found only in the northern tablelands of New South Wales, mainly the New England Range area on poor soil types.

CULTIVATION: A tree which is extensively cultivated in Australia and in California, because of its attractive foliage and neat, pyramidal habit of growth. Adapts to most soils, including limestone, where trees sometimes suffer from chlorosis (yellowing of the foliage).

E. nutans F. Muell.

RED-FLOWERED MOORT

DESCRIPTION: Although this species is usually a low bushy
mallee to 2.5 m high under natural conditions, in cultivation it is often grown as a single-stemmed small tree
with a very dense bushy crown, its width often as much
as its height of about 4 m.

The bark is smooth and light brown, ageing to grey
before deciduating. Leaves are alternate, thick, rather
short with a slender stalk, lanceolate to broad-lanceolate.
The flower buds are stalkless or on short pedicels in
umbels of up to seven, the umbel on a strap-like peduncle. The often reddish caps are dome-shaped and
narrower than the receptacle.

When the flowers open, normally in spring, they are
dark red with creamy anthers; occasionally the filaments
are pale red or cream. Fruits are cup-shaped or inverted
cone-shaped, with two opposite ribs forming a keel.

OCCURRENCE: Restricted to the south coast of Western
Australia from near Bremer Bay to the Ravensthorpe–
Hopetoun area.

CULTIVATION: A good screening or windbreak tree with
ornamental flowers. Suited to most soils including heavy
clay in areas receiving 300–600 mm of rainfall.

E. obliqua L'Hérit.

MESSMATE, MESSMATE STRINGYBARK

DESCRIPTION: A tall, normally erect tree, 30–65 m high under natural forest conditions, but more wide-spreading with lower branches where it is able to grow as a single specimen. The bark is rough, persistent, and fibrous, grey on the surface but brown beneath. Leaves are long and broad-lanceolate, a glossy dark green on both sides, and the new tips are reddish bronze.

Small creamy white flowers are produced abundantly in summer. The bud caps are short and conical. Fruits are cylindrical on short, stout stalks, the valves hidden.

The timber is hard and straight-grained and is milled extensively in Victoria and Tasmania.

OCCURRENCE: A widely distributed forest tree of south-eastern Australia and Tasmania from the cooler, mainly mountain areas where rainfall is 750–1250 mm annually.

CULTIVATION: Messmate is rarely cultivated, but has been included because of its natural occurrence in some urban areas near large cities, such as parts of the Mount Lofty Ranges near Adelaide and some outlying areas of Melbourne.

E. occidentalis Endl.

FLAT-TOPPED YATE

DESCRIPTION: This is a medium-sized, erect tree, 12–20 m high, with a branching, usually flat-topped canopy of foliage mainly over the top third of the tree.

A distinguishing feature of the tree is the thinly fibrous, flaky grey bark on the trunk and lower part of the main branches, and smooth white or cream bark thereafter. The leaves are mainly lanceolate on a relatively long stalk.

The flower buds are produced in umbels of up to seven, each bud on a short thick pedicel attached to a long flattened peduncle. The caps are long and conical-cylindrical, and the stamens are pale yellow. Flowering is normally in autumn and winter. Fruits are distinctly bell-shaped with protruding triangular valves.

OCCURRENCE: A common tree of the wheatbelt and along the south coast of Western Australia between Wagin and Israelite Bay. It favours alluvial flats subject to flooding.

CULTIVATION: An easily grown, drought-resistant and frost-resistant tree which has been frequently cultivated in Australia and overseas. Reasonably salt-tolerant. Good honey tree.

E. odorata Behr & Schldtl.

PEPPERMINT BOX

DESCRIPTION: This is a small to medium-sized tree or mallee, 7–15 m high, with fibrous, chunky, dark grey to black, rough bark on the lower parts of the tree, but smooth brown to grey bark on most of the branches.

It features narrow, lanceolate, dark green, oily leaves and numerous unbranched clusters of conical flower buds which open into creamy flowers, usually from autumn to early summer. The small fruits are cylindrical to hemispherical with hidden valves.

OCCURRENCE: Mainly a South Australian tree from areas in the 450–550 mm rainfall range, but extending just across the border into western Victoria. It favours undulating lowlands and is fairly common in parts of the Barossa Valley and the plains north of Adelaide and also in the Strathalbyn area. The variety name *angustifolia* has sometimes been used for a very narrow-leaved form of the species.

CULTIVATION: An attractive small to medium-sized tree, which usually produces an abundance of cream flowers. Easily grown and a good honey tree.

E. oleosa F. Muell.

GIANT MALLEE, RED MALLEE

DESCRIPTION: A mallee or spreading tree, 3–12 m high, with smooth, grey deciduous bark and a little rough, flaky bark at the base. This very widespread tree is botanically close to a number of other species and hybrids are not uncommon. There are also several described varieties.

The leaves are mainly lanceolate and deep green. The buds occur in stalked clusters, the bluntly conical or domed cap being narrower than, but about equal in length to, the torus. Flowers are creamy white to pale yellow, usually appearing in late winter and spring. Fruits are almost globular, narrowing at the orifice, with fragile, sharply pointed, protruding valves.

OCCURRENCE: Widely distributed throughout the mallee regions of southern Australia.

CULTIVATION: A very hardy, drought- and frost-resistant tree suited to most soils and situations in low to moderate rainfall areas. Cultivated in North Africa.

Nicolle (*Eucalypts of South Australia*, 1997) divides this species into three subspecies, two yet to be named.

E. orbifolia F. Muell.

ROUND-LEAVED MALLEE

DESCRIPTION: This is a mallee or small bushy or slender, tree up to 6 m high, but usually less, which features rounded or obcordate grey-green leaves and smooth reddish bark which curls off in longitudinal strips, eventually to reveal fresh pale green and cream bark. The reddish young branchlets are covered with a mealy bloom, as are the buds.

Bud caps are hemispherical-conical to conical, opening to expose creamy yellow stamens, normally in autumn and winter. The fruits are powdery grey, hemispherical or short and bell-shaped, the unopened valves projecting from the centre of the disc in similar fashion to the clapper of a bell.

OCCURRENCE: From the goldfields of Western Australia, with a smaller fruited, narrow-leaved form found in a few isolated populations of the Musgrave Ranges, South Australia, the Petermann Ranges, Western Australia, and the MacDonnell Ranges, Northern Territory. This form was first considered to be *E. websteriana* (page 290) and may eventually be given a new name.

CULTIVATION: This is an ornamental and unusual small tree which has been occasionally cultivated over a wide range of conditions in Australia from southern Queensland to Western Australia.

E. ovata Labill.

SWAMP GUM

DESCRIPTION: At its best this is a medium-sized, quite shapely tree to 15 m high, but under natural conditions is usually seen as rather a crooked tree of poor shape. The bark is rough and flaky over the lower trunk but is otherwise smooth and streaky, tan and grey, or of varying colours.

The mature leaves are ovate-lanceolate, rather glossy and wavy, the juvenile leaves much more rounded in shape. Buds are usually double-conical, three to 10 in the cluster, the caps variable, sometimes beaked. Flowers are white, appearing from autumn to spring. The fruits are distinctly conical with a flat disc, the valves about level with the rim.

OCCURRENCE: A tree mainly found in poorly drained flats or nearby slopes throughout many parts of south-eastern Australia, from New South Wales through southern Victoria to the wetter parts of South Australia. It is common in northern and eastern Tasmania.

CULTIVATION: A tree which is cultivated specifically because of its usefulness for waterlogged sites, including those which are mildly saline.

E. papuana F. Muell.
var. *aparrerinja* Blakely

(*Corymbia aparrerinja* Johnson & King, 1996)

(*Eucalyptus aparrerinja* Brooker, 1999)

GHOST GUM

DESCRIPTION: This tree, made famous through Aboriginal artists, is of variable size depending on habitat. It may be only a slender tree of 7 m, or an erect-trunked tree with spreading crown, to 25 m high. The smooth, pure white, lustrous bark, to which it owes its common name, is its most distinctive feature. Leaves are deep green and lanceolate, on pendulous brittle branches.

The buds are club-shaped with short, rounded caps, the white flowers usually appear in autumn or winter.

Fruits are papery and bell-shaped and are shed soon after maturing, making seeds of this species difficult to obtain.

OCCURRENCE: Found only in central Australia, mainly across the Northern Territory, but extending marginally across the borders of Western Australia and Queensland. It is often confused with the associated inland form of River Red Gum (*E. camaldulensis var. obtusa*—page 56).

CULTIVATION: Occasionally cultivated with success in Adelaide, but rarely grown in gardens.

E. papuana F. Muell, var. *papuana*, Cape York Ghost Gum, is a smallish tree from a restricted area of Cape York Peninsula and the islands north to Papua New Guinea. Its bark is grey and flaky at the base of the trunk.

E. petiolaris (Boland) Rule

EYRE PENINSULA BLUE GUM, WATER GUM

DESCRIPTION: Formerly included under *E. leucoxylon*, this small to medium-sized tree, usually 6–10 m high, may be straight, or of crooked, irregular habit. Bark is mostly smooth except for the lower trunk where it is a rough brownish-grey. The leaves are dark green, lanceolate to falcate, normally 80–140 mm long. The flowers which resemble those of *E. leucoxylon*, vary considerably in colour and may be cream, bright yellow, orange-red, pink or scarlet, with conical caps. Flowering is usually autumn through winter to spring. The fruiting capsules tend to be longer than those of *E. leucoxylon*, featuring a thickened stalk where it joins the capsule. Seedling leaves also differ in their long stalks.

OCCURRENCE: Restricted to south-eastern Eyre Peninsula in South Australia where it favours the banks of water-courses and gullies. It extends inland as far as the Cleve hills.

CULTIVATION: A useful, attractively-flowered, usually small tree, which is suited to most soils, including limestone, in a temperate climate. There is a form in cultivation which is very tolerant of saline soils.

Two colour forms are illustrated below.

E. phoenicea F. Muell

SCARLET GUM, FIERY GUM, GNAINGA

DESCRIPTION: This is a small tree to about 10 m high, with a slender, often crooked trunk, the crown wide-spreading, or narrow, and the foliage often sparse. Soft, scaly, persistent, brownish bark clothes the trunk and main branches but is smooth and white thereafter. The mature leaves are rather thick, lanceolate, 70–140 mm long by 10–25 mm wide. The flowers are spectacular, a vivid orange or crimson, in globular clusters formed from axillary umbels arranged in a circular fashion around the main angular peduncle. Buds are club-like, the caps bluntly conical and the fruiting capsules are also in globular clusters, each capsule resembling a long ribbed, earthenware vase or pot.

OCCURRENCE: Restricted to the Top End of the Northern Territory and extending into the Kimberleys in Western Australia, east of Gibb River. It favours poor skeletal or rocky soils on escarpments. There is also a small isolated occurrence north-west of Cooktown in Queensland.

CULTIVATION: Although not often cultivated, this tree has great appeal for northern gardens with well-drained soils. It is long-flowering, the flowers colourful and rich in nectar, and the tree's smallish size is well-suited to urban gardens.

Fruits

E. pilularis Smith

BLACKBUTT

DESCRIPTION: A medium-sized to tall, shaft-like tree 20–40 m high with brown or light grey, rough, fibrous bark persisting over part of the trunk. The upper trunk and branches shed their bark leaving it smooth and cream to white.

The mature leaves are lanceolate or falcate to 160 mm long by 30 mm wide, a dark glossy green, paler on the undersurface. White flowers, about 15 mm across occur in axillary umbels on strongly flattened peduncles about 15 mm long, the conical caps long and pointed. Flowering is in spring through summer. Fruiting capsules are 10–12 mm long and wide, rounded or cup-shaped, the valves slightly sunken below the rim.

OCCURRENCE: Extends along a narrow coastal band from near Gympie in Queensland to Eden in southern New South Wales. Soils and climate are variable from wet to fairly dry locations. Grows naturally in parts of Sydney.

CULTIVATION: An important fast-growing timber tree for eastern Australia and planted in many overseas countries. Too large for most home gardens but suited to park planting. The leaves are eaten by koalas.

E. pimpiniana Maiden

PIMPIN MALLEE

DESCRIPTION: This quite rare species never grows to tree stature, forming a multistemmed, spreading shrub 1–2 m high, and usually wider than its height. It features white or grey smooth bark throughout, thick, lanceolate to broad-lanceolate leaves up to 10 cm long, and masses of showy, cream or yellow (sometimes white) flowers in umbels of up to 11 in the leaf axils. Flowering may be irregular, but is mainly from July to November.

The buds, on a flattened peduncle usually 1 cm or more long, are pendulous, the torus long and conical to cylindrical, striate or faintly ribbed. The beaked caps are mostly slightly shorter than the torus. Fruits are faintly ribbed, cylindrical to somewhat bell-shaped.

OCCURRENCE: A South Australian mallee from scattered locations on the Nullarbor Plain and northwards to Maralinga.

CULTIVATION: An unusual shrubby species, particularly attractive when in flower. Suited to most well-drained soils in open situations where rainfall does not exceed about 600 mm annually.

E. platypus Hook. var. *platypus*

MOORT, ROUND-LEAVED MOORT

DESCRIPTION: This is mainly a small, stiff tree, 4–8 m high, with a dense rounded crown of thick, variable but usually elliptic to orbicular, olive green leaves. The bark is smooth, brown when fresh, but ageing to grey before it sheds in strips.

The flower buds are stalkless in clusters of up to seven on a thick, strap-like, curved peduncle. Caps are long horn-like and straight. The flowers are usually produced in spring and summer. These are a citrus yellow or white, and quite showy, but sometimes obscured by the dense foliage. Fruits are top-shaped, with several ribs.

OCCURRENCE: A tree from near the south coast of Western Australia, extending from around Albany east to Esperance and, in places, inland about 80 km.

E. platypus var. *heterophylla* Blakely is a coastal variety which differs in that it has pointed lanceolate to ovate leaves, usually white flowers, and smaller fruits.

CULTIVATION: A rapid-growing, hardy tree which is useful as an ornamental, a windbreak and a street tree. Withstands moderately saline soils as well as most others. The variety *heterophylla* is a good tree for planting near the sea and an excellent windbreak on farms because of its low and dense branching habit.

E. polyanthemos Schauer

RED BOX

DESCRIPTION: Normally a medium-sized, rather spreading, short-trunked tree 15–20 m high, but sometimes reaching larger proportions.

It features rough, shortly fibrous, light brown to grey bark throughout (occasional trees are smooth-barked) and broad ovate to oval blue-grey leaves. The juvenile leaves are blue and almost circular, the apex notched.

The small white flowers are produced in panicles in spring and summer. Bud caps are shortly conical. Fruits are small, pear-shaped, with deeply included valves.

OCCURRENCE: A fairly common tree of open woodlands in much of central Victoria and east Gippsland, extending along the inland slopes of the Great Dividing Range in New South Wales and to adjacent tablelands.

CULTIVATION: An attractive foliage tree for parks and large gardens where rainfall exceeds about 450 mm. The tree is cultivated in Europe and the USA for the juvenile foliage, which is used in the flower trade. Good honey tree.

E. baueriana Schauer, Blue Box, also features a dense crown of grey-blue broad leaves. It has distinctly conical or funnel-shaped fruits, but some botanists consider this tree to be only a variation of *E. polyanthemos*.

E. populnea F. Muell.

BIMBLE BOX, POPLAR GUM

DESCRIPTION: This is usually only a medium-sized, branching tree 10–15 m high, but it sometimes reaches 25 m. The grey bark is rough, short-fibred, and persistent to the smaller branches.

A feature of the tree is the broadly elliptic, poplar-like leaves on long slender stalks, which are mainly glossy with a lacquered appearance. However, forms with dull leaves also occur. The flower buds are produced in umbels on short erect peduncles, the caps shortly conical. Flowers are small and white, usually appearing in summer. The clustered fruits are small and hemispherical, with sunken valves.

OCCURRENCE: A common tree of inland south-eastern Queensland and north-central New South Wales, favouring heavy clay soils which are subject to waterlogging after heavy rains.

CULTIVATION: A good shade tree for heavy soils in areas of low to moderate rainfall.

E. porosa F. Muell. ex Miq.

MALLEE BOX

DESCRIPTION: Mallee Box is a small, often crooked or irregularly branched tree 8–10 m high, or a many-stemmed mallee to about 6 m. The bark is dark to mid-grey, finely fibrous or scaly over the trunk and lower branches, but grading to smooth higher in the tree.

The leaves assist in distinguishing the species because of their usually rather pale or lettuce green colour. They are narrow- to broad-lanceolate, wavy and shining. Bud caps are conical, blunt or pointed, and the flowers are white in small stalked umbels of three to seven. Flowering occurs from winter to summer. The fruits are pear-shaped with hidden valves.

OCCURRENCE: A species which is widespread in South Australia throughout the shallow calcareous soils which extend from the upper south-east to the Ceduna area on Eyre Peninsula. Extends into western Victoria and New South Wales. It is closely related to Peppermint Box (*E. odorata*—page 188) and some intergrading occurs.

CULTIVATION: A tree which is mainly grown because of its hardiness on difficult shallow limestone soils, where many other species struggle.

213

E. preissiana Schauer

BELL-FRUITED MALLEE

DESCRIPTION: A low, straggly, woody mallee, 2–3 m high, which is mainly a shrub and best treated as such in cultivation. It has smooth grey bark and large, thick, ovate, mainly opposite leaves with blunt or obtuse tips.

It is the abundant large, bright yellow flowers, mainly in three-flowered umbels on a thick peduncle, with often reddish, rounded or bluntly conical bud caps, which are the attractive feature of this plant. These are produced in late winter to late spring. The fruits which follow are large and bell-shaped, the valves enclosed and slightly below the rim.

OCCURRENCE: This shrub occurs along the southern coastal areas of Western Australia from the Stirling Range to Stokes Inlet, often in thickets and favouring stony soils.

An eastern form (var. *lobata*), with larger flowers and fruiting valves domed above the rim, occurs from Stokes Inlet to Esperance.

CULTIVATION: An ornamental flowering shrub which is easy to grow in well-drained soils, including limestone. Flowering is prolific if it is grown in an open sunny situation.

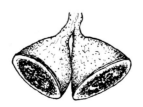

E. ptychocarpa F. Muell. *(Corymbia)*

SWAMP BLOODWOOD

DESCRIPTION: An upright leafy tree, normally 8–12 m high, with a wide-branching, drooping habit and rough, fibrous, flaky brown bark. The leaves are very large and broad, undulate, with the typical parallel veins of the bloodwoods.

The flowers are borne prominently in large heads above the foliage, either white, pink or a brilliant crimson, usually appearing in autumn months. Buds and fruits are neatly ribbed by eight longitudinal ribs, the caps being hemispherical with a short, blunt beak, and the fruits cylindrical to ovoid.

The timber of this species is particularly soft.

OCCURRENCE: This is a tree of the tropics, being found along the banks of streams and in other moist locations in the northerly parts of the Northern Territory and parts of the Kimberley region of Western Australia.

CULTIVATION: A spectacular flowering tree which is being grown with success in Queensland and the Northern Territory, where summers are hot and wet. It flowers when 3 to 4 years old. The authors have no evidence of the ultimate size to which it may grow under garden conditions.

E. pulchella Desf.
Syn. *E. linearis* Dehn.

WHITE PEPPERMINT

DESCRIPTION: This Tasmanian species is a most graceful tree, often slender, usually 7–10 m high, but occasionally larger when grown on rich soils. It normally has smooth white and grey deciduous bark, but sometimes patchy rough brown or grey bark is dominant on the trunk.

The very narrow, bright green leaves can be slightly pendulous or rather stiff, but always produce an attractive foliage effect. The buds are typical of the peppermints, small and club-shaped in axillary umbels, the caps hemispherical or slightly conical. Thick clusters of small white flowers appear in late spring, followed by small pear-shaped fruits.

OCCURRENCE: A tree of south-eastern Tasmania, common in the Hobart region, usually growing on poor stony soils of dolerite origin.

CULTIVATION: A very ornamental and graceful tree of moderate size which is well suited to suburban gardens of south-eastern Australia.

E. amygdalina Labill., Black Peppermint, is generally a larger tree, common throughout much of Tasmania. It is variable, however, and similar to *E. pulchella* in some narrow-leaved forms. Hybrids between the two species are not uncommon.

E. pulverulenta Sims

SILVER-LEAVED MOUNTAIN GUM

DESCRIPTION: This is a small, narrow, sometimes straggly tree to about 7 m high, which features silvery blue foliage on branches which often begin near ground level and grow horizontally. The bark, which is mainly smooth and waxy white, sheds to leave a smooth reddish surface beneath.

The silvery leaves are rounded or heart-shaped in opposite, stalkless pairs, more or less at right angles to the branches. Powdery buds and fruits in groups of three cluster along the branches in the leaf axils. The caps are beaked and hemispherical and the fruits also hemispherical or cup-shaped with a flat disc. The flowers are creamy white, appearing from spring to autumn.

OCCURRENCE: This is a rare tree, being restricted to only a few localities of the central and southern tablelands of New South Wales, including the Blue Mountains near Sydney.

CULTIVATION: An ornamental-foliaged tree which is best suited to acid soils and cool, moist situations but can be grown under warmer conditions where water is available.

E. perriniana F. Muell. ex Rodway, Spinning Gum, has similar but larger juvenile leaves and is cultivated for this feature. However, it eventually grows to about 8 m with narrow, lanceolate adult leaves.

E. pyriformis Turcz.

DOWERIN ROSE, PEAR-FRUITED MALLEE

DESCRIPTION: This is a slender-stemmed mallee, usually 3–5 m high, with smooth, grey-brown deciduous bark. The leaves are grey-green to blue-green, lanceolate to ovate-lanceolate, and rather small in the bluish-leaved form.

It is the spectacular flowers which are the feature of the tree. These are produced in threes on thick, pendulous pedicels and peduncles, a bright red or pink with yellow anthers; less commonly they are cream or yellow. The caps are conical or rounded, and these, along with the large inverted conical fruits, are conspicuously striated with many longitudinal ridges.

Flowering usually occurs in early winter to spring.

OCCURRENCE: This tree is an inhabitant of mainly sandy heathland, being found in the Goomalling area north-east of Perth and extending northwards in a narrow band to near the Murchison River.

CULTIVATION: A plant which can be extremely ornamental if trained to become a neat multistemmed mallee. It is relatively easy to grow in most temperate parts of Australia, but resents wet feet.

E. radiata Sieb. ex DC. subsp. *radiata*

NARROW-LEAVED PEPPERMINT

DESCRIPTION: At its best this is a lovely medium-sized erect tree 20–25 m high, often with a pyramidal shape, and with rough, grey, persistent, finely fibrous bark. It has most attractive foliage of narrow grey-green to blue-green thin leaves.

The flowers, which usually appear in spring and summer, are typical of the peppermints—small and numerous, white, in many-flowered umbels, the buds club-shaped. Fruits are pear-shaped or ovoid, with valves at rim level. The leaves are rich in oil and have been harvested for commercial purposes.

OCCURRENCE: Widely distributed throughout central and eastern Victoria, extending into southern New South Wales, favouring deep, moist soils. It is common in the upper Blue Mountains. Also found in Tasmania.

CULTIVATION: A good farm shade and shelter tree in areas of assured rainfall. It is used as a street tree in some Victorian country towns.

E. piperita Smith ssp. *piperita*, Sydney Peppermint, is also a common tree of the Blue Mountains and the sandy soils of Sydney's urban areas. It is a moderate to large tree and is of historical interest because it was the first eucalypt from which oil was distilled.

The subspecies, *urceolaris*, is similar, but a larger tree, differing in its distinctly urn-shaped fruits.

E. redunca Schauer

BLACK MARLOCK

DESCRIPTION: This is normally a low, slender-stemmed mallee, 1.5–4 m high, with a bushy canopy of dark green foliage and smooth brown to grey-brown bark which peels in ribbons. It sometimes grows to a tree 8–10 m high.

The leaves are narrow, lanceolate to falcate, alternate and relatively small. The long, narrow, conical, pointed flower buds on slightly flattened peduncles are claw-like in their later stages of development. They are produced in profusion, with sometimes 15 buds to the umbel, opening to reveal masses of creamy-coloured flowers, usually in summer. The fruits are cylindrical to top-shaped, with slightly protruding valve points.

OCCURRENCE: A widespread tree of south-west Western Australia, mainly in the wheatbelt in the 300–500 mm rainfall range.

CULTIVATION: An adaptable, easily grown small tree which is suitable for screening and windbreaks. Good flowering forms are ornamental when in bloom.

E. wandoo Blakely, Wandoo, is an erect, white-trunked tree to 30 m high which bears similar flower buds and fruits. It has been considered a tree form of the Black Marlock, and was once known as *E. redunca* var. *elata*. It occurs in higher-rainfall areas (400–750 mm) of south-west Western Australia.

E. regnans F. Muell.

MOUNTAIN ASH

DESCRIPTION: This is Australia's tallest tree, a giant shaft-like forest tree which grows over 100 m high, although more usually 50-80 m. The bark is rough, fibrous, and persistent on the lower trunk, this often being obscured by understorey plants, but smooth and deciduous thereafter, white or pale grey, shedding in long ribbons.

Mature leaves are long, narrow-lanceolate to lanceolate and curved, a deep green in colour. The white flowers appear in stalked many-flowered umbels; the bud caps are conical. Flowering is usually in summer and autumn. Fruits are hemispherical to pear-shaped with included valves.

The timber is hard and durable and is milled for flooring and construction purposes.

OCCURRENCE: A tree of the high-rainfall forests of Tasmania and eastern Victoria, with an outlier in the Otway Range.

CULTIVATION: Rarely cultivated, but a dominant tree of some national parks and natural forest areas, where it is much admired. It is a common tree of the Dandenong Ranges of Victoria, where it can often be seen in bush and other gardens.

E. rhodantha Blakely & Steedman

ROSE MALLEE

DESCRIPTION: This is a low, straggly mallee or shrub, 1–3 m high, distinguished by its large, rounded or heart-shaped, silvery grey stem-clasping leaves. The bark is smooth, grey-brown to pale grey.

The flower buds are also powdery grey, occurring in the leaf axils on distinct pendulous stalks, sometimes up to three in an umbel, but usually singly. Bud caps are conical or hemispherical with a pointed apex. The large flowers (5–8 cm across) are usually bright red with yellow anthers and may appear at any time. Fruits are woody, hemispherical or top-shaped.

This species is closely related to *E. macrocarpa* (page 158) which differs in its flowers, which are without pedicels, and its normally ovate leaves. Intermediate forms between the two species are known.

OCCURRENCE: In mainly sandy soils, extending about 80 km to the north and south of Watheroo in Western Australia. Average rainfall is 380–500 mm.

CULTIVATION: Suited to an open sunny situation in most soils but it resents those which are very limy. Has been successfully grown in Sydney where climate differs greatly from that of its natural habitat.

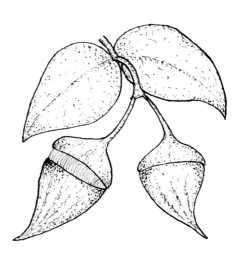

E. risdonii J. D. Hook.

RISDON PEPPERMINT

DESCRIPTION: Usually a small, slender tree of bluish white appearance, no more than 5–6 m high, but occasionally much larger to 12 m or so, with brown to green deciduous bark grading to mealy white on the smaller branches. Both juvenile and mature leaves are glaucous, opposite, perfoliate, and ovate-lanceolate to cordate in shape, the apex pointed.

The mealy, club-shaped buds and creamy white flowers appear profusely from the leaf axils in umbels of seven to 20, usually in October–November. Individual flowers are almost sessile, while the umbels are on a peduncle 1–2 cm long. Fruits are pear-shaped or hemispherical, 6–8 mm in diameter with a flat or slightly sunken disc and valves.

OCCURRENCE: A rare tree restricted to a small area near Hobart in Tasmania. It can be found naturally on the Government Hills at Risdon and near the Richmond–Hobart airport junction, on poor mudstone soils.

CULTIVATION: A small, ornamental, blue-foliaged tree which is grown in Tasmania and occasionally on the mainland, particularly in the cooler wetter south-eastern parts. It succeeds in the Adelaide area and appears to be generally hardy.

233

E. robusta Smith

SWAMP MAHOGANY

DESCRIPTION: This is a medium-sized, normally erect tree to about 20 m high, with rough grey, sometimes corky-looking bark, and a dense crown of large, glossy, handsome leaves. These are dark green, leathery, broad-lanceolate or ovate-lanceolate, with a prominent midrib and parallel veins.

The creamy white flowers appear in winter and spring in dense umbels on a long peduncle, and are displayed prominently above the foliage. The beaked, bulbous caps are creamy yellow or pink, and they and the flowers contrast well with the foliage. Fruits are cylindrical with slightly protruding valves.

Swamp Mahogany is closely related to Bangalay (*E. botryoides*—page 42) but is a superior flowering tree of smaller stature.

OCCURRENCE: An inhabitant of swamps and coastal lagoons never far from the sea. It is found in southern New South Wales, and north to south-east Queensland as far north as Fraser Island.

CULTIVATION: An ornamental tree suited to a range of conditions but particularly useful for soils subject to flooding. Extensively cultivated overseas in Hawaii and North Africa.

E. rossii R. T. Baker & H. G. Smith

SCRIBBLY GUM

DESCRIPTION: A small to medium-sized tree which features a smooth, white-barked trunk and branches when fresh, the older bark a patchy greyish-white marked with numerous insect scribbles. Leaves are grey-green, narrowly lanceolate to falcate, up to 150 mm long. The bud caps are small and hemispherical, fragile. White flowers appear in summer on small axillary umbels. Fruiting capsules are small, hemispherical, about 5 mm by 5 mm.

OCCURRENCE: The most widely distributed of the Scribbly Gums, extending over the inland tablelands of New South Wales from near the border of Queensland south to Wagga Wagga. A common, attractive tree in Canberra, where it grows naturally.

CULTIVATION: A handsome tree best suited to temperate areas of moderate rainfall on most well-drained soils, but resents those which are very limy. Frost hardy. An excellent landscape tree.

E. haemastoma Smith, *E. sclerophylla* (Blakely) L. Johnson & D. Blaxell, and *E. racemosa* Cav. are similar species called 'Scribbly Gum', all from Sydney and nearby, *E. racemosa* extending north along coastal areas to the Brisbane region. All species differ slightly in their buds and fruits.

E. dalrympleana
Maiden subsp. *dalrympleana*

MOUNTAIN GUM, WHITE GUM
CANDLEBARK GUM IN SOUTH AUSTRALIA

DESCRIPTION: Under favourable moist conditions this lovely tree grows to 30 m high with a long, erect, white-barked trunk and a rounded canopy of foliage high up. The bark is smooth and waxy, ageing to grey and reddish tones before deciduating. Occasionally some rough bark is present at the base of old trees.

Juvenile leaves are opposite, rounded and dull blue to green-grey, but become alternate, lanceolate to narrow-lanceolate and deep green at maturity. The buds and fruits are produced in threes on a short peduncle, the caps conical and of roughly equal length to the torus. Fruits are ovoid with a domed rim and protruding triangular valves. Flowers are white, appearing in late spring and summer.

OCCURRENCE: Cool, fertile areas of the Mount Lofty Ranges in South Australia, but more common in mountainous country of Victoria, New South Wales and Tasmania.

CULTIVATION: A highly ornamental medium to large tree best suited to cool, moist conditions and acid soils.

NOTE: This tree was formerly included as *E. rubida* Deane and Maid., which the South Australian form was thought to be until 1997 (Nicolle, *Eucalypts of South Australia*).

E. rugosa (R. Br.) Blakely

KINGSCOTE MALLEE

DESCRIPTION: This is a compact, bushy mallee species which seldom exceeds 4 m high with smooth, grey-brown, deciduous bark throughout. The leaves are thick, lanceolate, grey-green to grey-blue.

The buds occur in short axillary clusters on a rather thick, flattened peduncle. Both caps and torus are ribbed, the caps hemispherical with a short beak, and much shorter than the torus. Flowers are creamy white, usually appearing in summer months. The fruits are more or less pear-shaped, ribbed, with pointed protruding valves.

OCCURRENCE: Mainly a coastal mallee, endemic to South Australia, where it extends from the Coorong to lower Yorke and Eyre Peninsulas. Common on southern Kangaroo Island.

CULTIVATION: An attractive, easily grown, shrubby species which is suited to most conditions in areas of low to moderate rainfall. It is especially useful for locations near the sea.

E. conglobata (R. Br.) Maiden, Cong Mallee, is a thick-leaved bushy mallee from South and Western Australia which is also useful for difficult coastal sites and limy soils. It is distinguished by its thick stalkless buds and fruits, and striated, conical caps about as long as the torus.

E. salmonophloia F. Muell.

SALMON GUM

DESCRIPTION: This medium-sized tree normally grows erect to no more than 20 m high, with a flattish or rounded crown of glistening green leaves. The fresh bark is smooth and salmon or brownish orange, but it ages to pale grey with brown patches, shedding in flakes. The tree can be distinguished by its fresh bark and shining, dark green, lanceolate to falcate leaves.

The small creamy flowers are produced in umbels of up to 11; the bud caps are hemispherical or sometimes slightly conical. Flowering is variable but is usually from spring to autumn. The small rounded or pear-shaped fruits have slender, pointed valves protruding from the centre of the orifice. Fruits quickly shed their seeds after maturing.

OCCURRENCE: A widely distributed tree of the wheatbelt and goldfields areas of south-west Western Australia. However, most of the Salmon Gums have been cleared from the cereal-growing regions.

CULTIVATION: A fine, rapid-growing tree for low to moderate rainfall areas, and suited to most soil conditions. Good honey tree.

E. salubris F. Muell. var. *salubris*

GIMLET

DESCRIPTION: Gimlet is an erect, branching tree which can reach 24 m, but is commonly no higher than 12–15 m at maturity. It normally has a rounded crown of shining, narrow-lanceolate green leaves and distinctive red-brown or greenish brown, shining, smooth bark and yellowish young branchlets. In some trees, particularly when young, the trunk is spirally fluted, giving rise to its common name.

The flower buds, which are often reddish, are in umbels, normally with short thick pedicels and a thick, slightly flattened, sometimes twisted peduncle. Caps are long and dome-shaped, the sides almost parallel, and flowers are cream, appearing mainly in summer and autumn. The fruits are hemispherical on a thick stalk with protruding valves.

OCCURRENCE: A common tree of the Western Australian goldfields, often in pure stands or in association with other species such as Salmon Gum. It extends through the wheatbelt but is mainly cleared from these areas. Rainfall is a low 200–380 mm.

CULTIVATION: A tough, easily grown, medium-sized tree which is best suited to dry or moderately dry conditions. Good honey tree. Eventually kills most plant life beneath its canopy.

E. salubris F. Muell. var. *glauca* Maiden, also from the goldfields of Western Australia, is a mallee featuring glaucous branches and larger, glaucous buds and fruits.

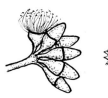

E. sargentii Maiden

SALT RIVER MALLET

DESCRIPTION: This is a small to medium-sized low-branching tree, mostly under 10 m high, with smooth, shining brown fresh bark and, normally, a little rough flaky bark at the base of the main trunk. Young branchlets are red, and foliage is dense. The leaves are alternate, and narrow-lanceolate to linear-lanceolate.

The creamy white flowers appear in spring, being produced in up to seven-flowered umbels on slender pendent stalks. The bud caps are long, cylindrical and pointed, often reddish in colour. Fruits are long, pear-shaped or cylindrical cup-shaped, with pointed, slightly protruding valves.

OCCURRENCE: A fairly restricted tree from a small area east of Perth in the Cunderdin – Lake Mears – Hines Hill – Wyola Siding vicinity. Rainfall is 300–380 mm.

CULTIVATION: An easily grown tree in most soils in areas of under about 650 mm of rainfall, but particularly useful for salt-affected soils. Eventually restricts plant life beneath its canopy.

E. scoparia Maiden

WALLANGARRA WHITE GUM

DESCRIPTION: This is a particularly ornamental tree because of its slender habit, white or mottled pale grey smooth bark, and very narrow, drooping foliage. It normally grows 9–12 m high.

   The leaves are long, narrow and pendulous, a lustrous deep green. Flower buds occur in short umbels on a slender straight peduncle, the caps usually hemispherical with a small beak. The flowers are small and white, appearing in summer, autumn, or winter depending on seasonal conditions. Fruits are ovoid with a prominent, raised, hemispherical disc.

OCCURRENCE: A rare tree which is restricted to granite hills on both sides of the New South Wales – Queensland border in the Wallangarra area.

CULTIVATION: A tree which is much sought after for ornamental planting. It is an adaptable tree but is sometimes unreliable without known cause, preferring well drained soils and assured rainfall. Of variable habit, some forms being stiffer and less ornamental and often much larger in stature. These appear to be hybrids between this species and *E. camaldulensis*.

E. sepulcralis F. Muell.

WEEPING GUM

DESCRIPTION: This is a most unusual tree, commonly growing up to 8 m high with a slender trunk only 5 or 6 cm
in diameter. The slender, drooping branches and trunk
are clothed by a smooth, powdery white bark. Leaves are
narrow, linear-lanceolate to narrow-lanceolate, olive
green or sometimes partly glaucous.

The buds and flowers are produced on slender, pendulous, powdery grey pedicels and long peduncles, the bud
caps conical and the stamens cream or pale yellow.
Flowering occurs in summer. The fruits are large and
urn-shaped, powdery grey-green at first, but ageing to
grey with a net-like pattern on the surface.

OCCURRENCE: A Western Australian tree found in a small
area between Hopetoun and Ravensthorpe in hills near
East Mount Barren and the Eyre Range, although it was
originally recorded from east of Esperance. Soils are stony
or sandy.

CULTIVATION: This tree has no value for shade or screening,
but is sometimes grown for its unusual habit. It is adaptable, but prefers well-drained non-limy soils.

E. pendens Brooker, Badgingarra Mallee, is an ornamental, thin-stemmed mallee to about 5 m high, with a slender, weeping habit, glaucous branches and prominently
ribbed, rounded fruits. Occurring in sandy heathland
between Gin Gin and Dongara, Western Australia, it
resembles *E. sepulcralis*, in mallee form.

E. sessilis (Maiden) Blakely

FINKE RIVER MALLEE

DESCRIPTION: This is a small, straggly mallee or shrub to about 3 m high with smooth grey deciduous bark. The leaves, on erect stalks, are thick, broad-lanceolate and grey-green.

The distinctive feature of the tree is the normally reddish, sessile buds in clusters of up to seven. These have a beaked conical cap and a hemispherical torus, both prominently ribbed. Cream flowers, which contast well with the red buds, usually appear in autumn and winter. Fruits are ribbed and feature a prominent erect ring surrounding the projecting valves.

E. pachyphylla F. Muell., Red-budded Mallee, differs only in the buds, which are in threes on thick pedicels and peduncle.

OCCURRENCE: *E. sessilis* is restricted to inland ranges of Central Australia, mainly the MacDonnell Ranges and nearby hillsides.

E. pachyphylla occurs in deep red sands of arid Central Australia (in Western Australia, South Australia, Queensland, and Northern Territory) at sparse locations.

CULTIVATION: Both species are shrubby plants with attractive buds and flowers. They have been successfully cultivated in Adelaide on calcareous soils and in drier country towns in South Australia.

E. sideroxylon Cunn. ex Woolls

RED IRONBARK, MUGGA

DESCRIPTION: In cultivation, this is normally an erect tree of medium size, 10–15 m in height, although specimens are known more than 30 m high. It is characterised by its distinctive dark grey to black, deeply furrowed, hard rough bark which persists to the smaller branches. The narrow foliage is grey-blue and provides a handsome contrast to the trunk.

The flowers, which appear in autumn and winter, hang in clusters of usually seven, either creamy white, bright pink, or in intermediate colours, and are quite showy. Bud caps are short and conical or hemispherical with a blunt beak, and the fruits are ovoid or pear-shaped with hidden valves. The timber is red, hard and durable.

OCCURRENCE: From north-eastern Victoria through the western slopes of the Great Dividing Range to southern Queensland. Also west of Sydney to the Blue Mountains.

E. tricarpa L. Johnson & K. Hill, also Red Ironbark, differs in its three-flowered inflorescences. It is the well-known ironbark of the Victorian goldfields, as well as south-eastern Victoria and southern coastal New South Wales.

CULTIVATION: Extensively cultivated, both species have proved adaptable to a wide range of soils and conditions throughout much of Australia.

E. socialis F. Muell. ex Miq.

RED MALLEE

DESCRIPTION: This widespread species is variable in form, usually a multistemmed mallee 5–8 m high, with a light canopy of greyish lanceolate leaves. Bark is mainly smooth and pale grey, with persistent rough bark at the base. Young branchlets are red. Leaves and twigs may be covered with a waxy bloom.

The juvenile or seedling leaves are sessile in opposite pairs, grading from very narrow at the base to broad-lanceolate.

Flowering is profuse, the pale lemon flowers in stalked umbels appearing from winter to summer. A distinctive feature is the long yellowish bud cap resembling an elf's cap. Fruits are rounded or slightly urn-shaped, with long, pointed, protruding valves which soon fracture.

OCCURRENCE: Widespread throughout the mallee regions of Australia Several close species confuse identification.

CULTIVATION: An easily grown small tree, best suited to areas of low to moderate rainfall. Good honey tree.

E. eucentrica L. Johnson & K. Hill, Inland Red Mallee. From south-western South Australia, where it is widespread from the Gawler Ranges westwards and northwards and into the Great Victoria Desert, extending into Western Australia and the Northern Territory. It is a similar tree and features showy yellow flowers, blue-grey leaves and powdery white buds and branchlets. A small tree which thrives in sandy or limy soils.

E. spathulata Hook. subsp. *spathulata*

SWAMP MALLET

DESCRIPTION: This distinctive tree, normally 6–10 m high, is easily recognised by its thick linear leaves which form a dense dark green canopy of foliage. The branches begin low on the trunk and are usually ascending. Bark is smooth and coppery brown, ageing to grey-green before deciduating.

The buds are produced on short pedicels in umbels of up to seven on a slightly flattened peduncle, the caps often reddish brown, oblong-cylindrical, with a rounded apex. Flowers are creamy white, appearing from spring to summer. Fruits are cup-shaped or hemispherical with protruding, pointed valves.

OCCURRENCE: A Western Australian species found near lakes and depressions over much of the south-west in the 350–500 mm rainfall range, from Wongan Hills to Ravensthorpe.

CULTIVATION: An extensively cultivated, rapid-growing, adaptable tree which is particularly useful for poorly drained, including mildly saline, soils. Because of its heavy crown, it is inclined to blow over in heavy soils where root growth is shallow. Eventually it restricts plant growth beneath its canopy.

E. spathulata Hook. subsp. ***grandiflora*** (Benth.) L. Johnson & D. Blaxell, is a larger-flowered form with a dense, low or mallee habit of growth. It is found over the more eastern extremities of the range.

E. steedmanii C. A. Gardner

STEEDMAN'S GUM

DESCRIPTION: This tree is small, rarely growing more than about 8 m high, but distinctive because of its habit of producing numerous ascending branches from low on the trunk to form a very symmetrical, dense, umbrella-like or flattish crown. The bark is smooth and brown, or sometimes grey-brown.

The leaves are narrowly elliptic to lanceolate and rather short. Flower buds are produced in threes on long angular pedicels and peduncles. The floral receptacle is four-winged and square-sided and the cap is pyramidal. The flowers usually open in summer, the stamens being cream or yellow, but occasionally pink or red. Fruits are similar to the floral receptacle, but larger, with protruding pointed valves.

OCCURRENCE: This Western Australian species is virtually unknown under natural conditions but was formerly collected in the Lake Grace area in sandy soil, rainfall about 300 mm. It is an endangered species.

CULTIVATION: The tree is commonly grown as a farm windbreak or shelter tree and for roadside and street planting because of its shape. It is easily grown in most soils in areas of low to moderate rainfall.

E. stoatei C. A. Gardner

PEAR GUM, SCARLET PEAR GUM

DESCRIPTION: This is a slender, erect or sometimes low-branching stiff-foliaged tree, 4–6 m high. The trunk is slender and clothed with smooth, grey, deciduous bark. Leaves are thick, oblong or elliptic-ovate, with an abrupt, pointed apex. The tree is easily distinguishable by its prominently ridged, red to greenish yellow, pear-shaped buds and fruits, produced singly on a pendulous peduncle. These clothe the tree all at the same time. The bud caps are shortly conical and much narrower than the torus. Stamens are short and bright yellow. Flowering occurs at odd times throughout the year, but more profusely over summer months.

OCCURRENCE: A rare tree found in a restricted area east and north–east of Ravensthorpe in Western Australia, to south of Pyramid Lake, favouring gravelly soils.

CULTIVATION: Although this tree is quite commonly cultivated in Australia, its stiff habit and foliage are not particularly ornamental and tend to offset the attraction of the buds, fruits and flowers. It is easily grown in heavy, as well as light, soils.

E. stricklandii Maiden

STRICKLAND'S GUM

DESCRIPTION: This is mainly a small tree, 6–8 m high, branching from low on the trunk, with large, thick, rather stiff leaves. The bark is powdery white on the smaller branches, extending to the flower buds, and a smooth coppery brown on the trunk and larger branches. On older trees there is some flaky, rough grey bark at the base. Young leaves are large, broad, ovate, sometimes mealy, but mature leaves are long and lanceolate.

The sessile flower buds are produced in umbels of up to seven on a thick, broad, flattened powdery white peduncle. Bud caps are yellow and dome-shaped. Flowers appear in large, thick clusters over the summer months, a showy bright yellow or yellow-green. Fruits are bell-shaped. A rare red-flowered form is also cultivated.

OCCURRENCE: A tree of the Western Australian goldfields, from Kalgoorlie to Norseman, where rainfall is only 250–280 mm annually.

CULTIVATION: An ornamental small flowering tree, particularly for dry areas, which is suited to almost any soil, including mildly saline. A useful honey tree.

E. tenuiramis Miq.
Syn. *E. tasmanica* Blakely

SILVER PEPPERMINT

DESCRIPTION: A small to medium-sized upright tree to 25 m high which features glaucous foliage and smaller branches, the young growth normally a purplish blue. It sometimes occurs with pendulous branches, this form being particularly ornamental. The bark is deciduous and is usually a patchy grey, grading to white on the upper branches.

It is closely related to *E. risdonii* (page 232) and its stem–clasping silvery blue juvenile foliage is very similar, making young specimens difficult to distinguish. The mature leaves are alternate, elliptic to lanceolate, and up to 12 cm long.

Buds are glaucous and are produced in thick axillary umbels, the caps short and slightly conical or pointed-hemispherical. The flowers are creamy white and appear in late spring. Fruiting capsules are pear-shaped with slightly sunken discs and valves.

OCCURRENCE: A Tasmanian species which is quite common in the Hobart area and the south-east of Tasmania, favouring poor mudstone soils.

CULTIVATION: This tree is frequently cultivated in Tasmanian cities, particularly in public plantations, but is rarely seen outside that State. Cool, moist conditions would appear desirable.

E. tereticornis Smith

FOREST RED GUM

DESCRIPTION: This is a large, upright tree to 45 m high, normally of good shape with an open, rounded crown. The bark is smooth, deciduating in large flakes, mottled grey or multicoloured. Some rough bark may occur at the base. The mature leaves are a glossy green, thick, long and narrow-lanceolate.

The tree is best identified by its long, conical bud caps, from which it derives its specific name. Flowers are white, appearing mainly in summer, and fruits are small and rounded with prominent, protruding, triangular valves, similar to those of the River Red Gum (*E. camaldulensis*—page 56).

OCCURRENCE: A tree of wide distribution throughout the east coast of Australia, extending from Gippsland in Victoria to Cape York and on into New Guinea. It favours flat, riverine habitats, but is also found on hill-sides, sometimes in a form with larger buds and fruits.

CULTIVATION: An easily grown tree over a wide climatic range. It is a naturally occurring species in many areas of Brisbane.

E. terminalis F. Muell

(Corymbia)

DESERT BLOODWOOD

DESCRIPTION: A small to moderate-sized tree often seen with several irregular trunks. The bark may be rough throughout or only on the lower trunk, tessellated and light brown with orange-red patches where the outer flakes have shed. The mature leaves are lanceolate, featuring in a light-foliaged crown. In a good year, flowers appear in conspicuous, usually creamy-white terminal panicles, in autumn/winter. The bud caps are white or cream, hemispherical to shallowly conical, and the fruits are large, an elongated urn-shape.

OCCURRENCE: This is a dominant and widespread tree across inland Australia, extending to the north-west coast of Western Australia, east to inland of the Dividing Range in Queensland, north to southern Arnhem Land, and south to just across the South Australian border.

CULTIVATION: An adaptable and attractive smallish tree, suited to a range of soils and climates, from semi-dry monsoonal in the north to arid and semi-arid temperate in the south. Several, somewhat similar, but less common Bloodwoods occur in Central Australia and there has been some confusion over this tree's identity.

E. tessellaris F. Muell. (*Corymbia*)

CARBEEN, MORETON BAY ASH

DESCRIPTION: Carbeen is usually a moderately tall, erect tree, 20–25 m high, although on poor soils it can be seen in a more stunted form to about 12 m. It is distinguished by its short stocking of persistent dark grey bark which cracks into small segments (tessellated) and the smooth cream or whitish bark on the upper trunk and branches. The crown is slender and drooping, and the long, narrow leaves are dull green.

Panicles of attractive white flowers are normally produced in summer. The bud caps are flatly conical or beret-shaped and the cup-shaped fruiting capsules are thin-walled and easily crushed.

OCCURRENCE: A common tree of mainly eastern Queensland, including the Brisbane area, extending a short distance into northern New South Wales. Grows to near the shoreline in north Queensland. Also found in Papua New Guinea.

CULTIVATION: An attractive, graceful tree which is particularly suited to tropical areas but is grown successfully as far south as Adelaide in the better soil areas.

E. tetragona (R. Br.) F. Muell.

TALLERACK, SILVER MARLOCK

DESCRIPTION: One of the shrubby mallees, 2–3 m high, usually a straggly bush but noted for its lovely silvery grey-blue foliage and mealy white buds, stems and bark. The older bark becomes grey to brownish, shedding in strips.

The large, thick leaves are oval and opposite, on white, square-sided stems. Flowers are in threes on a flattened, angular peduncle, the buds mealy white and club-shaped on short angular pedicels. Flowers are white or cream, appearing mainly in summer. Fruits are grey-white, more or less urn-shaped, with a square disc and four ribs, the valves enclosed.

OCCURRENCE: This is a common shrub of the south coastal regions of Western Australia from well east of Esperance to the Stirling Range near Albany, favouring sandy soil in heathland. There is an outlier along the north coast near Badgingarra.

CULTIVATION: If trained to a bushy shrub, this is a very ornamental foliage plant which is suited to most soils. Like other blue-leaved species, it often suffers from caterpillar attack.

E. tetraptera Turcz.

SQUARE-FRUITED MALLEE, FOUR-WINGED MALLEE

DESCRIPTION: This is a small straggly tree or shrub rarely above 3 m high, with very large, thick glossy leaves — the largest leaves found on any eucalypt. These are leathery and broad-lanceolate to elliptical. The bark is smooth, usually grey.

This plant is easily distinguished by its large, shining red, single flower buds on a twisted, pendent peduncle. The buds are square-sided with four fleshy wings or ribs. The caps are roughly conical and the stamens pinkish red, appearing mostly in the spring, but also at any time of the year. Fruits are large, woody, quadrangular, with four wings.

E.erythrandra Blakely & Steedman is a very similar plant distinguished by its much smaller red flower buds, and fruits which are not so prominently winged.

OCCURRENCE: Both species are found in the heathlands of the south coast of Western Australia, *E. tetraptera* extending from the Stirling Range to Israelite Bay and *E. erythrandra* in the Ravensthorpe district.

CULTIVATION: These plants are more unusual than ornamental, although the flowers and buds of *E. tetraptera* can be quite showy. They are best grown as a shrub and are suited to most soils in low to moderate rainfall areas.

E. torelliana E. Muell. *(Corymbia)*

CADAGA

DESCRIPTION: A dense, short but shapely tree in cultivation, the crown low-branching and of regular shape. Although reaching to over 30 m. high in its native northern Queensland, as a cultivated tree it is rarely seen exceeding half this height. Bark is unusual being a smooth green over most of the tree.

The leaves too, are unusual. They are light to mid-green, broadly ovate, hairy and wavy. These are the intermediate leaves, the true adult leaves, which are narrowly lance-shaped, rarely being seen.

The small white flowers are borne in terminal panicles, mainly in threes on the panicle, in late spring–early summer, sometimes producing a second flush of flowers. They collapse quickly and can be disappointing. Buds resemble small green boiled eggs in an egg cup. Fruits are spherical, 9–14 mm across.

OCCURRENCE: A north Queensland tree where it is found from about Ingham to Mossman on the seaward slopes of the ranges and undulating country of the Atherton Tableland. Summer rainfall is very high.

CULTIVATION: Despite its tropical natural habitat this tree is particularly adaptable in cultivation and is one of the most popular garden eucalypts in southern Queensland, often in dry locations of the Darling Downs. It is successful in Adelaide where the climate is the exact opposite of north Queensland.

E. torquata Leuhm.

CORAL GUM, COOLGARDIE GUM

DESCRIPTION: Usually a small but sometimes a medium-sized, rough-barked tree, 6–11 m high, with a dense rounded crown of dark grey-green foliage. The rough, dark grey bark is slightly fibrous and becomes smooth grey-brown on the smaller branches. Leaves are dull, alternate and falcate or lanceolate.

The red, pink or cream flowers are distinctive and beautiful, appearing over long periods at any time of the year. These hang down in thick clusters on thin round pedicels attached to a drooping peduncle. The buds are usually red or orange, the torus and the horn-like cap being corrugated at the base. Fruits are cylindrical with an expanded, corrugated base.

OCCURRENCE: A tree of the Western Australian goldfields area, most common in the Coolgardie district.

CULTIVATION: One of the most extensively cultivated small trees in Australia as an ornamental or street tree. Easily grown in most conditions, it is particularly good for dry inland areas where the flowers are usually more intensely coloured.

E. × 'Torwood'

A GARDEN CULTIVAR

DESCRIPTION: This tree, so-named because it is considered to be a spontaneous hybrid between *E. torquata* (page 280) and *E. woodwardii* (page 292), is a variable tree which sometimes is closer to the more compact habit of *E. torquata*, but at other times displays the tall, more slender form of *E. woodwardii*.

It is usually small to medium-sized, with rough brown bark grading to smooth on the upper branches and dull, broad, green to blue-green leaves. Variations continually occur according to the parent seed.

The tree is noted for its prolific and showy flowers which can be bright yellow or, more usually, yellow-orange to orange. These display features common to both species, again with variations from tree to tree. They are produced abundantly from winter to summer. Fruits vary according to the flower variations.

OCCURRENCE: The tree is believed to have originated in a Kalgoorlie nursery from seedlings raised from seed of cultivated specimens of parent species.

CULTIVATION: A very hardy, rapid-growing tree which thrives in most soils in areas of low to moderate rainfall. Popular in dry, country areas where the flowers are normally magnificent.

E. transcontinentalis Maiden

REDWOOD, BOONGUL

DESCRIPTION: Usually a slender, single-stemmed tree 8–20 m high with a rounded canopy of foliage, but sometimes occurring in mallee form. The bark is mostly smooth and white to pale grey, older trees occasionally carrying some rough, fibrous bark at their base. Mature leaves are glaucous or grey-green and lanceolate, usually 8–14 cm long, and the thin young branchlets are often red.

Flowering is profuse, mostly in spring months, the flowers being pale lemon yellow and stalked in umbels of usually seven. Bud caps are hemispherical narrowing to a long, horn-like protuberance. Fruits are more or less globular, narrowing at the top. Timber is reddish, hard and durable.

Both fruits and flowers are virtually identical to those of the Red Mallee (*E. socialis*, page 256), but Redwood can be distinguished at the seedling stage by its broader, decurrent (i.e. forming a wing along the stem) seedling leaves, these being similar to those of Merritt (*E. flocktoniae*, page 110).

OCCURRENCE: A fairly common tree of the Western Australian wheatbelt and goldfields areas, usually growing in red sandy loam.

CULTIVATION: Although this is an ornamental small to medium-sized eucalypt, it is not well known in cultivation. Outside its natural distribution there is little evidence of its reliability as a cultivated tree.

E. viminalis Labill. subsp. *viminalis*

MANNA GUM, RIBBON GUM

DESCRIPTION: This is a variable tree depending on conditions, but it is most often a tall, shaft-like tree to 35 m high, with smooth, mainly white bark and a little rough bark at the base. The old bark is shed in long ribbons which hang from the branches before falling. Leaves are long, narrow and lanceolate.

The flower buds occur in threes on a short peduncle, the cap being conical and about equal in length to the torus. Flowers are white, appearing mostly from late spring to autumn. Fruits are spherical to conical, with a domed or convex disc and protruding valves.

This is one of the eucalypts on which the Koala feeds.

OCCURRENCE: A widely distributed tree in Victoria, Tasmania and south-eastern New South Wales, as well as the Bass Strait islands. It favours deep fertile valleys and the edges of streams, although in the Mt Lofty Ranges near Adelaide, South Australia, it is sometimes a much smaller tree on steep hillsides. The Rough-barked Manna Gum, *E. viminalis* subsp. *cygnetensis* Boomsma, is much more common in South Australia.

CULTIVATION: A fine tree for deep, moist soils and cool conditions.

subsp. *cygnetensis*

E. watsoniana F. Muell.

LARGE-FRUITED YELLOW JACKET

DESCRIPTION: An upright, fairly open-crowned tree of small to medium size which features scaly or papery yellowish brown bark, a feature of all of the eucalypts commonly known as yellow jackets or yellow bloodwoods. The leaves are dull green, rather long and tapering.

The large cream flowers occur in showy panicles towards the ends of the branchlets, normally in spring to early summer. As conspicuous as the flowers are the unopened buds, which are a glossy pale green, the caps being green or yellowish, and resembling a Scottish beret. Fruits are large, up to 2 cm long, and narrowly urn-shaped.

A tree which is very popular with birds, particularly honeyeaters and lorikeets.

OCCURRENCE: From the catchment areas of the Dawson and Burnett Rivers in south-eastern Queensland, where it favours dry, open forest and both clay and sandy soils.

CULTIVATION: An attractive moderate-sized tree which is not particularly well known in cultivation. It grows successfully in the red-brown earths commonly encountered in many urban areas of Adelaide.

E. websteriana Maiden

WEBSTER'S MALLEE

DESCRIPTION: A compact, dense-foliaged small tree to 6 m high, with small, rounded, grey-blue to grey-green leaves. The bark is smooth and yellow-green when fresh but ages to a coppery red, curling off in thin longitudinal strips. Leaves are dull, obovate with a notched apex, or obcordate. The new growth is often pinkish.

The pale lemon flowers occur in up to seven-flowered umbels on thin, erect pedicels and peduncle. The buds are pinkish grey and ovoid, the caps shallowly dome-shaped with a slight point. Flowering occurs in autumn and winter. Fruits are rather like tops and smaller than those of the very similar Round-leaved Mallee (*E. orbifolia*—page 192).

OCCURRENCE: A Western Australian endemic from the Coolgardie District, occurring from Menzies to the Fraser Range, where it favours sandy or stony soils near granite outcrops.

CULTIVATION: This is an ornamental small tree which is suited to planting in small gardens. It grows well in most soils in areas of low to moderate rainfall.

E. woodwardii Maiden

LEMON-FLOWERED GUM

DESCRIPTION: At its best this is one of the loveliest of the flowering gums, growing tall and slender with long, drooping, flexuose branches. The branches, trunk and buds are covered with a waxy white powder, which contrasts with the broad, thick, mealy grey-blue leaves and bright yellow flowers. On mature trees, there is often some rough bark at the base. Height is usually 10–15 m.

The attractive, frosted white flower buds with hemispherical, beaked caps and the large clusters of cascading brilliant yellow flowers are produced over long periods, normally throughout the warmer months of spring and summer, but at other times also. Fruits are bell-shaped and mealy white.

OCCURRENCE: A tree restricted to a small area east of Kalgoorlie where rainfall is under 250 mm annually.

CULTIVATION: Extensively cultivated in dry inland towns where it grows strongly and flowers profusely. Thrives on limestone soils. In colder wetter climates and fertile soils it is inclined to grow spindly and to suffer from leaf-eating predators.

293

E. youngiana F. Muell.

LARGE-FRUITED MALLEE, OOLDEA MALLEE

DESCRIPTION: This is a straggly, shrubby mallee, or sometimes a small branching tree 8–10 m high, with smooth,
grey deciduous bark and a little rough persistent bark at
the base. The leaves are thick and rather stiff, mostly
broad-lanceolate, and greyish green in colour.

The tree is most easily distinguished by its very large
buds, flowers and fruits on short, thick stalks in umbels
of three. The flowers, which normally appear from late
winter to late spring, are especially striking, and are
cream, yellow, pink or crimson.

Bud caps are conical or hemispherical, ribbed with a
distinct beak. The fruits are broader than they are long,
and prominently ribbed, with a vertical collar surrounding the protruding valves.

OCCURRENCE: A species from dry inland areas of western
South Australia and similar country in eastern Western
Australia, favouring red sands.

E. kingsmillii (Maiden) Maiden & Blakely subsp. *kingsmillii*, Kingsmill's Mallee, is a closely related small mallee
which features a more compact habit and smaller cream
flowers. A Western Australian endemic from the arid
north as far as the Hamersley Range. The subspecies
alatissima Brooker & Hopper, from the red sands of the
Great Victoria Desert in South Australia and Western
Australia, features colourful orange-red flowers.

CULTIVATION: Both species are ornamental small trees
because of their flowers. They can be grown in most
well-drained soils, in areas of low to moderate rainfall.

Bibliography

BEADLE, N. C. W., EVANS, O. D. & CAROLIN, R. C. *Flora of the Sydney Region.* Reed, Sydney, 1973.

BLAKELY, W. F. *A Key to the Eucalypts*, 2nd edn. Forestry and Timber Bureau, Canberra, 1955.

BOOMSMA, C. D. Contributions to the Genus Eucalyptus from South Australia. *South Australian Naturalist* vol. 48 no. 4, June 1974.

BOOMSMA, C. D. *Native Trees of South Australia* (Woods and Forests Department of South Australia, Bulletin No. 19). Government Printer, Adelaide, 1972.

BROCK, J. *Top End Native Plants.* John Brock, Darwin, 1988.

BROOKER, M. I. H., & KLEINIG, D. A. Field Guide To Eucalypts, vol. 1 (revised edn.), 1999, vol. 2, 1990, & vol. 3, 1994, Inkata Press, Melbourne & Sydney.

CHIPPENDALE, G. M. *Eucalyptus Buds and Fruits.* Forestry and Timber Bureau, Canberra, 1968.

CHIPPENDALE, G. M. *Eucalypts of the Western Australian Goldfields (and the Adjacent Wheatbelt).* (Forestry and Timber Bureau) Australian Government Publishing Service, Canberra, 1973.

CLIFFORD, H. T. *Eucalypts of the Brisbane Region*, The Queensland Museum & S.G.A.P. (Queensland), Brisbane, 1972.

FAIRLEY, ALAN, & MOORE, PHILIP *Native Plants of the Sydney District*—An Identification Guide, Kangaroo Press and S.G.A.P.-N.S.W. Ltd., Sydney, 1989.

FORESTS DEPARTMENTS, WESTERN AUSTRALIA *Selected Flowering Eucalypts of Western Australia.* Forests Dept of WA, Perth, n.d.

GARDNER, C. A. *Trees of Western Australia* (Department of Agriculture of Western Australia, Bulletins nos 1078, 1096, 2007, 2015, 2029, 2123, 2195, 2755, 2780, 2827, 2846, 2904, 3021, 3125). Reprinted from *Journal of Agriculture of Western Australia*, 1952–1963.

GRAY, A. M. Tasmanian Eucalypts. *Australian Plants* vol. 5 no. 39, June 1969, pp. 115–123.

HOLLIDAY, I. *A Field Guide to Australian Trees*, 3rd edn. Reed New Holland, Sydney, 2002.

JESSOP, J. P. & TOELKEN, H. R. (eds) *Flora of South Australia*, 4th edn, part II. Government Printer, Adelaide, 1986.

JOHNSON, L. A. S., & HILL K. *Telopea, vol. 6* (2–3), March–Sept. 1995, Sydney, 1995.

KELLY, S. *Eucalypts*, vol 1. Thomas Nelson, Melbourne, 1969.

KELLY, S., CHIPPENDALE, G. M. & JOHNSTON, R. D. *Eucalypts*, vol. 2. Thomas Nelson, Melbourne, 1978.

NICOLLE, DEAN *Eucalypts of South Australia*, Dean Nicolle, Adelaide, 1997.

GLOSSARY

alternate: placed at different levels — referring to the position of successive leaves on the branchlets.

anther: the pollen-bearing part of a stamen.

apex: the tip of an organ, such as a leaf.

axil (adj. axillary): the angle between a part and its parent body — e.g. a leaf and the main stem of a plant.

campanulate: bell-shaped.

capsule: a dry fruit formed from a multi-chambered ovary.

cordate: heart-shaped.

corymb (adj. corymbose): an inflorescence with flowers approximately at one level owing to varying pedicel lengths. The lowermost or outside flowers which open first have longer pedicels than the upper ones.

crenate: having the margins bordered by blunt or rounded teeth.

cylindrical: shaped like a cylinder, with sides more or less parallel.

deciduous: of leaves or bark, shed at the end of the growing season.

decurrent: of, e.g., a leaf, having its base continuous along the stem in the form of a wing.

disc: the portion of the fruit between the staminal ring and the valves.

elliptic: shaped like an ellipse — referring to the shape of leaves.

elliptic-oblong: shaped roughly halfway between elliptic and oblong.

falcate: sickle-shaped; flat, curving, and tapering to a point.

filament: the stalk of an anther.

glabrous: smooth, without hairs.

glaucous: bluish green, with a powdery bloom.

globular: rounded or ball-shaped.

hypanthium: enlarged floral receptacle enclosing the ovary; torus.

included: enclosed, not projecting.

inflorescence: the flower-bearing system.

lanceolate: lance-shaped; elongated, narrowing at both ends, and broadest below the middle.

lateral: occurring at the side.

lateritic: of a soil, containing laterite or ironstone.

lignotuber: conspicuous swelling at the base of a stem at or below soil level — e.g. as in a mallee eucalypt.

linear: long and narrow with more or less parallel sides.

mallee: eucalypt with several stems arising from a common rootstock.

margin: edge.

midrib: the main central vein of a leaf, especially when raised.

obcordate: inversely heart-shaped (i.e. with a broad notch at the apex).

oblanceolate: inversely lanceolate, being broadest above the middle.

oblique: slanting or with unequal and asymmetrical sides.

oblong: with sides more or less parallel except at the base and the apex.

oblong-cylindrical: cylinder-shaped with the sides nearly parallel except at the base and the apex.

obovate: inversely ovate; egg-shaped and broadest above the middle — referring to a two-dimensional structure such as a leaf.

obtuse: rounded-ended or blunt.

operculum: a cap, as in *Eucalyptus* buds.

orbicular: circular.

ovary: the part of the flower containing the ovules which, after fertilisation, develops into the fruit.

ovate: egg-shaped and broadest below the middle — referring to a two-dimensional structure such as a leaf.

ovoid: egg-shaped and the broadest below the middle — referring to a three-dimensional structure such as a fruit.

panicle: a raceme in which instead of single flowers there are clusters of flowers with pedicels or stalks

pedicel: the stalk of an individual flower.

peduncle: the stalk of a cluster of flowers, or of an individual flower if this is the only member of the inflorescence.

perfoliate: having the growth of the leaf blade continued around the stem so that the stem appears to grow through the leaf or pair of leaves.

pyriform: pear-shaped.

raceme: a simple inflorescence with a central axis producing stalked flowers along its length.

receptacle: tip of a floral stem bearing floral units which form the flower; the base of the flower (in *Eucalyptus* often called the torus).

rim: circular scar on the fruit where the bud cap was attached.

rugose: wrinkled.

sclerophyll forest: forest dominated by evergreen sclerophyllous trees (trees with hard-textured leaves such as *Eucalyptus*).

sessile: without a stalk.

spathulate: spoon-shaped, more or less oblong to circular at the apex, but having a long, narrow base — e.g. referring to the shape of a leaf.

stamen: male part of a flower, consisting of a filament (stalk) and a pollen-bearing anther.

staminal rim or ring: the scar on the eucalypt fruit where the stamens were attached.

striate: having fine longitudinal lines, such as are created by the vein structure of some leaves.

terete: needle-like, elongated and round in cross-section.

tessellated: divided into small square or oblong scales.

torus: floral receptacle, hypanthium.

truncate: cut off squarely and abruptly, as in the apex of some leaves.

umbel: an arrangement of pedicellate flowers all arising from the same point on the floral axis or peduncle.

umbrageous: providing shade.

undulate: wavy (up and down in a different plane).

valve: one segment of a fruit which naturally opens at maturity, usually containing seeds.

vein: strand of conducting tissue in a leaf.

venation: the way in which veins are arranged.

INDEX OF COMMON NAMES

INDEX OF SCIENTIFIC NAMES

ABOUT THE AUTHORS

Ivan Holliday is a South Australian author who began writing about Australian plants in 1964. Since then he has written 13 books, five in the Field Guide series of which three have been with Geoffrey Watton.

A Life Member of the Field Naturalists Society of South Australia and of the Australian Plants Society (SA region), he is a keen conservationist and a lover of the Australian bush. He has travelled extensively throughout Australia to study and photograph its flora and is a frequent contributor to Australian plant journals.

Geoffrey Watton has lived in Adelaide all his life and was employed as a survey draftsman from 1945 until his retirement in 1985. He became interested in Australian plants in 1958, joined the Australian Plants Society and has been a keen grower ever since. His special interest is growing Western Australian species and he has made many trips to that State to study and photograph its native plants.

The revised and updated third edition of *A Field Guide to Australian Trees* by Ivan Holliday has recently been published by Reed New Holland.